SIGN GALLERY 3

from the editors of *Signs of the Times*

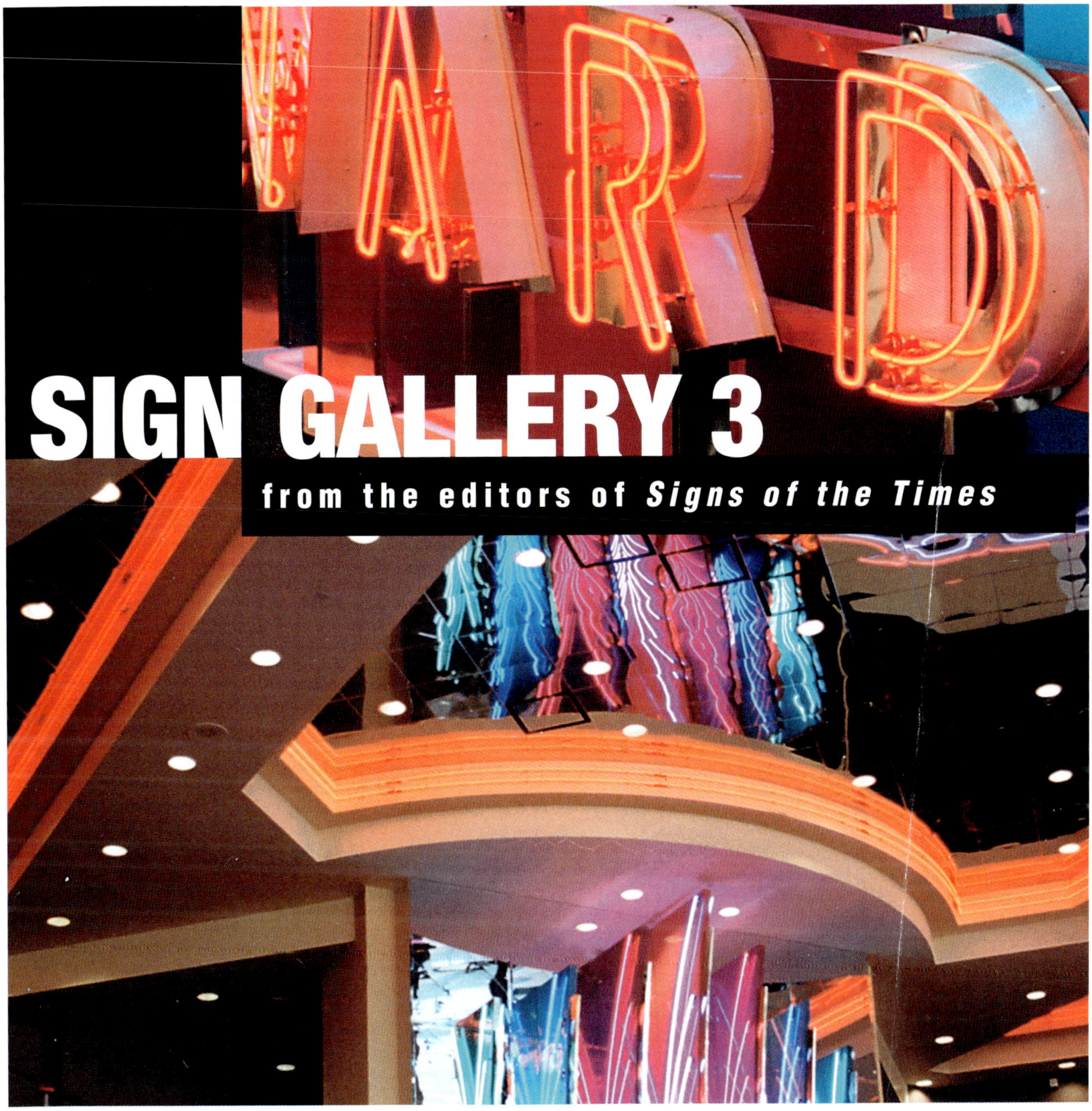

ST PUBLICATIONS
CINCINNATI, OHIO

ISBN: 0-944094-37-6

Published by:

ST Publications, Inc./Signs of the Times
Book Division
407 Gilbert Avenue
Cincinnati, Ohio 45202

Tel. 513-421-2050
Fax 513-421-6110
E-mail: books@stpubs.com
www.stpubs.com

Distributed to the book and art trade by:

HarperCollins International
10 East 53rd Street
New York, NY 10022-5229
Fax 212-207-6927

Book design by Jeff Russ

Printed in China

10 9 8 7 6 5 4 3 2 1

The sign projects presented in this book are drawn from the winners of the annual *Signs of the Times* Commercial and Electric Sign Design Competitions. The competitions are open to any sign designer or fabricator, and submissions from around the world are welcome. For more information, contact the Competition Editor of *Signs of the Times* at the phone, fax or address on page 2, or download the rules and entry forms at SignWeb.com.

SIGNS OF THE TIMES

Technological innovations continue to affect the design and installation of electric signs. Large-format digital imaging has nearly achieved complete photorealism, as has LED technology used in giant moving picture displays. The scale of many of the signs in this edition are truly immense, particularly as Las Vegas casinos continue to one-up each other in competition for the world's largest and most exciting signs. These improvements have not replaced the more traditional electric signs, however, especially for more conventional uses. Backlit awnings and neon signs and architectural graphics continue to be in demand, especially by retailers and restaurant operators seeking a more classic look.

Fabricator
Young Electric Sign Co. (YESCO)
Las Vegas
(702) 876-8080
Designer
Lisa Adams
YESCO
Client
The Venetian Resort Hotel Casino

Illuminated by No. 4-triphosphor, warm-tone, cove neon and two antique brass-plated lamps, this double-faced monument sign for the Venetian Resort Hotel Casino features smooth, aluminum faces, with a faux-marble paint finish.

Beveled, gilded copy made of Sign•Foam® high-density urethane is recessed into routed areas of the faces. The lion in the center of the fiberglass scroll is also gilded.

Fabricator
    Lockwood Sign Group
    Beltsville, MD
    (301) 937-1121
Client
    Restaurants at the Lake

This 21 × 38-ft. wide, aluminum and steel restaurant display will surely satisfy your appetite.

The sign's letters are halo-lit with 6500 white, EGL neon, pumped using a Eurocom processing station. Neon is also used on the sign's top collars, while the bottom collars comprise up-and-down Phillips halogen lights.

The center ribbon is suspended within a 3 × 4-in. rectangular, aluminum-tube frame using ¼-in. stainless-steel threaded rods. Stainless-steel hardware and ¼-in. stainless-steel aircraft cable support the frame. All finished components are welded and painted using Matthews' acrylic polyurethane paint.

Supporting the sign are 16-in.-diameter steel poles installed on anchor-bolt foundations. Atop the poles are pennants that rotate with the direction of the wind.

Original Logo Signs: Freestanding

Fabricator
Landmark Sign Group
Chesterton, IN
(219) 762-9577
Designer
VOA
Chicago
(312) 554-1400
Client
Chicago Shakespeare
Theater
Selling Price
$128,000

Measuring 59 ft., 10 in. × 8 ft., this freestanding, double-face sign comprises a cabinet, letters and background, all fabricated from aluminum and painted using DuPont Centari® colors.

More than 1,200 flashing, chasing and scintillating, 11-watt incandescent bulbs are used on the perimeter of the sign cabinets and inside the "Shakespeare" letters. Adding further illumination to each letter are 250 end-lit fiberoptic cables (2mm). "Chicago" and "Theater" are lit with 15mm amber/gold neon and feature a 3-mil, high-performance, vinyl backdrop for daytime reading.

The bottom of the sign incorporates changeable, transparent, internally illuminated Mylar® graphics to indicate what is showing at the theatre.

Fabricator
Shaw Sign & Awning
Fort Collins, CO
(970) 493-6244
Designer
Dallas Griffin
Shaw Sign & Awning
Client
Palmer Design Center
Selling Price
$13,000

Letters were routed into the back of the 2-in. acrylic body, then the entire back was sandblasted. An aluminum strip was placed around the left side, while a 2-in. aluminum pipe went around the outside. Purple neon accents the sign, which was placed in an oval shaped brick base. The finishing top circle was constructed using an aluminum cage with applied cutout, flat aluminum letters.

Fabricator
ARTeffects Inc.
Bloomfield, CT
(860) 242-0031
Designer
ARTeffects Inc.
Client
Tapas Restaurant

This sign is 8-in. plate textured aluminum with a clear lens over open-face channel letters, served with a cooking pot channel letter that includes a face printed on a GerberEDGE®. ARTeffects sprinkled in downlighting on half-inch, acrylic-sprayed triangles and downlighting on the supporting pole.

Fabricators
  John Connor and Tommy Jarvis
  United Studios Sign Group
  Longwood, FL
  (407) 831-3484
Designers
  Bob Lee and Chad Harmon
  United Studios Sign Group
Selling Price
  $27,000

With a welded-aluminum cabinetry construction, this 12-foot-tall display has an 8 × 8-ft., multi-dimensional, reverse-lit logo incorporating the printer's registration mark with the numeral "4." Four perforated-metal, colored inserts recessed into the inner openings of the registration mark indicate process colors, and multi-colored neon illuminates the inserts from behind the outermost face. The outer back "4" element stands 2 inches away from the base cabinetry and and is illuminated by recessed white neon. The "Four Graphics" copy in the angled, projecting support is waterjet-cut, ½-inch-thick, push-through white acrylic; the support is finished in royal blue to match the building accents and has "Nova" pearlescent highlights.

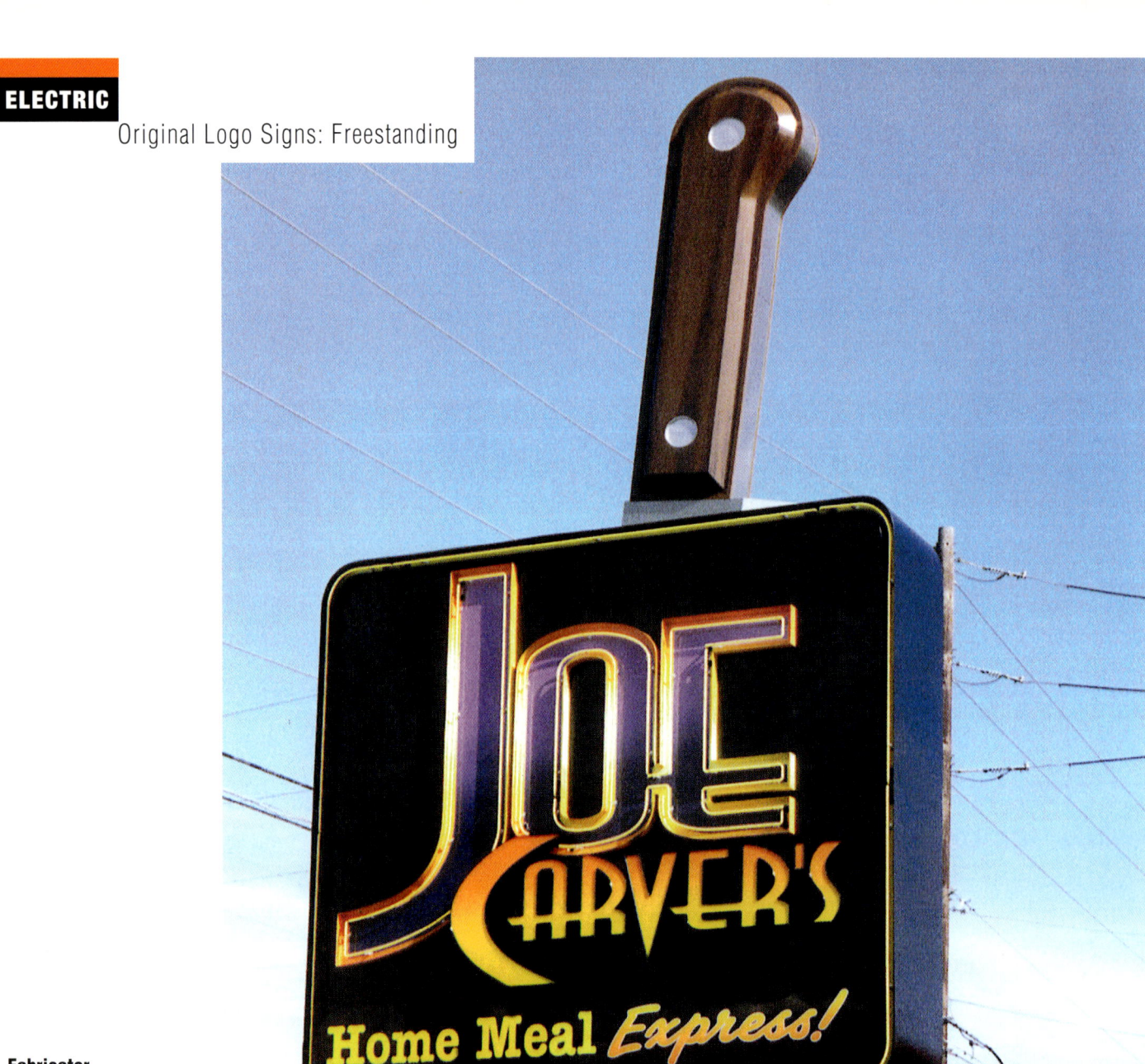

Fabricator
Sekula Sign Corp.
DuBois, PA
(814) 371-4650

Designers
Mike Newcomer
Sekula Sign Corp.

M.H. Gartner
Impact Advertising
Williamsport, PA
(717) 323-7741

For this cutting-edge sign, two steel columns allow a narrow knife blade that meets structural requirements. The $3\frac{1}{2} \times 8$-ft. Lexan® polycarbonate knife handle is attached to a structural aluminum-and-steel framework. Various sign parts include: an exposed neon border; 4- to 7-foot channel letters with exposed neon for "Joe," each custom-sprayed using Akzo Nobel Grip Gard® polyure-thane; "Carver's" fabricated out of $1\frac{1}{4} \times 2\frac{1}{2}$-ft. channel letters with internal neon illumination and custom-finished and blended acrylic faces; and "Home Meal Express," which features $1\frac{1}{2} \times 10$-ft. letters with fluorescent illumination through reverse-sprayed acrylic faces. The structural frame of the 10×12-ft. sign cabinet is welded aluminum, angle-reinforced by structural steel.

Fabricator
Arrow Sign Co.
Oakland, CA
(510) 533-7693

Designer
Charlie Stroud
Arrow Sign Co.

Client
San Pablo Intl. Marketplace

Possibly the largest gateway sign in California, this 138-ft.wide welcome mat spans four lanes of traffic with 11,000 pounds of steel trusses. The perforated, painted, aluminum truss holds 15- and 22-in. high open-pan channel letters that include exposed gold neon. The green and blue globe logo was backlit and enhanced by a 5-ft. purple neon star, which hangs slightly from the middle of the truss, leaving a 37-ft. clearance for the cars beneath.

Original Logo Signs: Freestanding

Fabricators
Missouri Neon/Visiontech
Springfield, MO
(417) 862-1778

Small Creations
Southlake, TX
(817) 379-6468

Designer
Chris Braun
Missouri Neon/Visiontech

With 14-foot-long animated feet on one side and a 13-foot-long animated arm on the other, this double-faced sign for the new Yakov Smirnoff Comedy Theater is really busting into Branson — Missouri, that is. Measuring 30 feet high and 27 feet wide overall, the sign also features an electronic display with a three-line, 13-foot wedge-base design. "Yakov" is fabricated out of open channel letters with electronic contractors.

Fabricator
Graphic Systems Intl. Inc.
Greensboro, NC
(800) 779-2891

Designers
Leigh Brinkley (logo)
Brinkley Design
Charlotte, NC
(704) 372-8666

Ryan Crutchfield & Assoc.
Greensboro
(336) 279-8399

Zoo Design Staff
North Carolina Zoological Park
Asheboro, NC
(336) 879-7452

Selling Price
$50,000

Fabricated from .125 aluminum sheet, the North Carolina Zoological Park's sign — measuring 7 feet, 4 inches tall, 52 feet wide and 4 feet, 10 inches deep — incorporates rolling hills, playful forms and colors in a unique design. Ambient internal neon illuminates the sign between all panel layers, and external ground floodlights illuminate from below. The sign's exterior was acid-etched, primed and finished in Matthew's acrylic polyurethane paint; a concealed engineered-steel tube frame supports all layers and the front radius panel.

Original Logo Signs: Mounted

Fabricator
Federal Sign
Las Vegas
(702) 739-9466
Designer
Sue Deveny
Federal Sign

For the Blues Legends Hall of Fame at the Horseshoe Hotel & Casino, Federal Sign was charged with concocting a note-able identity that would be visually overwhelming. To meet the challenge, Federal fabricated a 28-foot saxophone with illuminated musical notes in clear-red neon mounted on a gold-finished raceway. Lamps indicating the musical lines chase out from the "sax" to simulate flowing music. The "Blues Legends" letters are box channel letters with exposed clear-red neon. The small cabinets down through the glass brick wall are low-relief sculptures of individual blues legends, halo-lit with white neon.

Fabricator
International Sign & Design Corp.
Largo, FL
(727) 541-5573

Designers
International Sign & Design Corp.

Ace Architects
Oakland, CA
(510) 452-0775

Several elements make this guitar gallery's signage sing: two animated guitar players, six double-faced headstocks and two deep FRP guitar awnings with illuminated "Guitar Gallery" signs. The two animated guitar players have internal steel structures clad with routed .250 aluminum; outer surfaces of perforated-metal aluminum overlays; and 15-millimeter exotic neon glass for illumination. One player's arm is animated via a Dynapac H2O oscillator; the other's guitar strings move via a standard cam animator. The headstocks have similar construction, featuring perforated metal, vinyl graphics and exotic neon glass. All six are animated using a cam animator in a north-to-south chase sequence. The "Guitar Gallery" signs are aluminum letters with 12-millimeter exotic neon glass on the faces.

Original Logo Signs: Mounted

Fabricator
Claude Neon, a Div. of the
Jim Pattison Sign Group Ltd.
Dorval, Quebec
(514) 856-7756
Designer
Diane Fafard
Claude Neon
Selling Price
$32,000

You don't need to be an optician to appreciate this eye-luminating sign. One set of 16-foot-high, red open-channel letters housing red neon and mounted on steel make up the vertical sign; the 25½-foot-long, 3-foot, 3-inch-high curved sign features a painted-blue steel structure, decorative tubing and red open-channel letters with red neon lighting. Blue incandescent fixtures housed in circular, painted-yellow steel structures create the "optical illusion" of dimension.

Fabricator
International Sign & Design Corp.
Largo, FL
(727) 541-5573

Designers
International Sign & Design Corp.

Ace Architects
Oakland, CA
(510) 452-0775

Channel letters for "Magnetron" are self-contained, feature 15-millimeter, ruby-red neon glass, and are attached to a wavy support structure fabricated from a rolled-aluminum pipe and tube. Other features include: three rings fabricated out of aluminum with three 15-millimeter, ruby-red neon rings; a globe fabricated from FRP; and an aluminum magnet and lightning bolts. Additionally, the magnet has multiple rows of animated neon behind the red and yellow plexiglas acrylic faces.

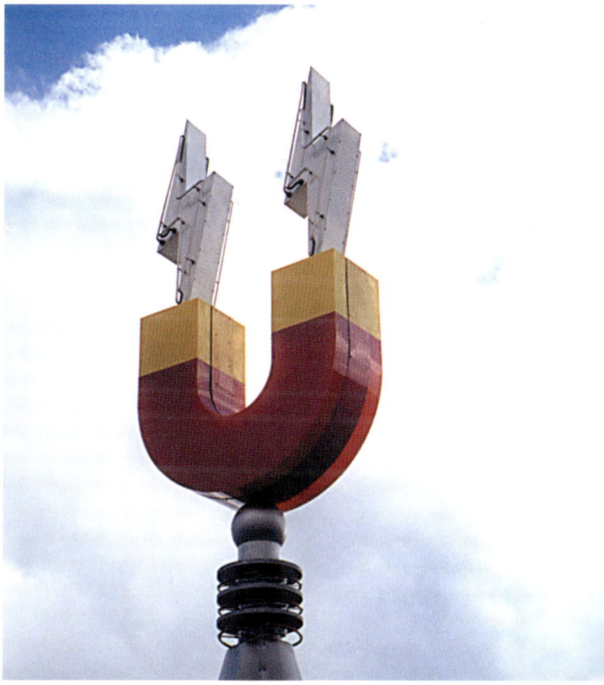

Original Logo Signs: Mounted

Fabricator
National Sign
Seattle
(206) 282-0700
Designer
Ken Krumpos
Seattle
Client
Seattle Art Supply

Censoring with discretion — with the city zoning restrictions in the historical section of downtown Seattle a concern, National Sign was asked to provide an appealing image that commanded attention.

DaVinci's "Vitruvian" man was screenprinted onto a painted aluminum panel and illuminated indirectly from the sides of the "Seattle Art Supply" fabricated acrylic word-box. The designers intended the classic ruby-red neon circle to merge the print with modern technology, almost acting as a target. The attachment plates were concealed with an arcing aluminum cover and decorative stainless steel turnbuckles imported from Germany.

Fabricators
Andy Brown and Ian Hain
United Studios Sign Group
Longwood, FL
(407) 831-3484
Designer
Bob Lee
United Studios Sign Group
Selling Price
$8,000

Because mall criteria prohibited generic projecting signs, Ultraneon created this sign as part of a dimensional element that extends around the corner to the main corridor, thereby gaining more exposure. The 18-inch-high, red-aluminum band, which ends in a pin-mounted spiral, creates the illusion of weaving in and out of storefront glass. Cantilevering with stainless-steel decorative pipe, the satin-black sign cabinet has a 3-D "Q" incised into the cube's alcove and 1-inch, waterjet-cut, push-through acrylic copy. An industrial-finished background refracts purple-neon edge lighting from within the cube to backlight the "Q."

Fabricator
Ultraneon Sign Co.
San Diego
(619) 569-6716
Designer
Graphic Solutions
San Diego
(619) 239-1335
Selling Price
$8,000

"Ceramic Cafe's" colorful logo is fabricated from aluminum and Sign•Foam® HDU. The reverse-channel letters have halo-lit neon and painted Sign•Foam caps to give the letters a baked-ceramic look. The painted palette has Sintra® expanded PVC paint-color spots with matching exposed-neon overlays.

Original Logo Signs: Mounted

Fabricator
National Sign
Seattle
(206) 282-0700
Designer
Ken Krumpos
National Sign
Client
Rock Salt Steakhouse

This 8 × 12-ft. sign adds spice to the exterior of the Rock Salt Steakhouse. The display's acrylic-faced channel letters are painted a gradation of yellow, while the "Steakhouse" copy is routed out of the background and backed with acrylic.

The sign's backdrop is an aluminum cabinet with a custom color blend. Running the length of the building on either side of the entry signage, the satin-black mesa graphics are cut from heavy-gauge aluminum and offset from the graduated color background. The mesas serve double-duty, concealing a raceway holding fluorescent lamps that shine upwards to halo-light the "sky."

Fabricator
Planet Neon
Novi, MI
(248) 348-8150

Designers
Forbes Management
Detroit
(313) 961-6451

Carmine Martone
Farmington Hills, MI
(248) 699-2000

Client
Gem Theatre

A jewel among marquee signs, this 6-ft., 10.5-in. × 16-ft., 2-in., projecting display advertises the Gem Theatre. The double-face sign incorporates a custom-shaped aluminum cabinet and painted graphics. Exposed neon and marquee bulbs provide illumination.

Fabricators
Ad-Art Electronic Sign Corp.
Stockton, CA
(209) 931-0860

Designer
AAD Interiors
Scottsdale, AZ
(602) 277-2703

Client
Ruby's Dinette

Fabricating this sign was no short order. Developed for a diner at Las Vegas' McCarran Intl. airport, the 12 ft., 7-in. × 10 ft., 4-in. aluminum display reflects the restaurant's neo-art-deco/aviation theme.

The "Ruby's" channel letters feature red returns, R&H #2793 red acrylic faces and red trim cap. "Dinette" comprises acrylic push-through letters, which are surfaced with polished, cut aluminum for halo illumination. Painted white, the sign's recessed aluminum background has a raised red border.

The simulated, five-cylinder "aircraft engine" has a formed, red, polycarbonate "cowl," illuminated with five sections of clear red neon that flash in alternating sequences. Silver-film "cylinder" graphics are applied to the face of the black, recessed "engineer" area. A formed, red, polycarbonate "spinner" is used on the stationary "propeller," which features painted, red-striped blades of FCO brushed aluminum.

Fabricator
  Federal Sign
  Las Vegas
  (702) 739-9466
Designer
  Sue Deveny
  Federal Sign
Client
  Tin Pan Alley

This 16 × 2 ½-ft. sign may look rusted, reused and run-over, but thats what the client ordered. Reverse pan channel letters with 15 mm/30 MA clear red neon illumination is mounted on treated corrugated metal painted to simulate old weathered/rusty metal. "Weathered" warehouse style lights on 2-in. rolled "rusted" pipes hold low watt bulbs so the light doesn't wash out the neon. The "Y" is flat cut–out aluminum, decorated as the others, but swings back and forth with a motion actuator. Exposed neon steadily burns. Federal Sign finished the sign with dark grey vinyl "tracks" across the metal.

Fabricators
Robin Smith
John Connor
United Studios (USID)
Longwood, FL
(407) 831-3484

Designer
Bob Lee
United Studios

Client
Yab Yum/The Globe

Selling Price
$7,830

Fabricator
  National Sign
  Seattle
  (206) 282-0700
Designers
  Kay Rice
  National Sign

  Wes Design
  Seattle
Client
  Coho Café
Selling Price
  $20,000

The client's desire for a sign that would reflect its unique menu and atmosphere matched perfectly with National Sign's ability to create a sign that was out of the norm. The results: big chunky open pan channel letters, cutout forks instead of salmon swimming upstream and eye-catching colors in a 7 × 8-ft., 6 in. sign.

Fabricator
Neon Products Ltd.
Vancouver, British Columbia
(604) 215-5526
Designer
Marla Hanson
Neon Products Ltd.
Client
WYSIWYG

Giving passersby the eye is a 12-ft.-
tall, custom-shaped, frameless-alu-
minum cabinet with routed lettering
backed with white acrylic. A circular
cabinet with an acrylic face and applied digital imaging completes the
structure. The sign's lettering and circular topper are internally illuminated.

Fabricators
    Planet Neon
    Novi, MI
    (248) 348-8150

    Alexander Forbe
    Incite Design
    Detroit
    (313) 921-7333
Designer
    Chuck Veres
    Planet Neon
Client
    C-POP

This art gallery opted for a fabricated stainless-steel awning with matching hardware components. In addition to a frosted, tempered-glass roof, the structure features an aluminum box sign with push-through acrylic lettering.

Fabricators
Federal Sign
Las Vegas
(702) 739-9466

CD Display
Las Vegas
(702) 263-4995

Designer
Sue Deveny
Federal Sign

Client
Paris Las Vegas Hilton

The Paris Hotel wanted an interior slot display similar to a model for the main pylon sign. To illuminate this 5-ft. balloon with two sets of light-filled letters and lighted rope and still have it constantly rotating, Federal Sign used side-glo fiberoptics instead of neon for the ropes and housed the light source within the balloon. The "basket" consists of four 40 × 25-in. plasma screens with hand carved rope and ribbon. The overall height is 17 feet.

Fabricator
Claude Neon, Div. of Jim
Pattison Sign Group
Quebec
(514) 856-7756
Designer
Diane Fafard
Claude Neon
Client
Quebec Loisirs
Selling Price
$8,897

Measuring 7 ft., 4 in. × 11 ft., 6 in., the aluminum pylon shown here features a 3-D globe molded in plastic and red-painted books made from galvanized sheet metal. The structure's aluminum cut-out letters are filled with ½-in. clear plastic and covered to the edges with blue vinyl. Internal fluorescent lamps and perimeter blue neon provide the sign's illumination. Incandescent goose-neck lamps afford additional lighting.

Fabricator
  Mikohn Lighting & Sign
  Las Vegas
  (702) 739-6789
Designers
  Mikohn Lighting & Sign

  Atlandia Design
  Las Vegas
  (702) 792-4600
Selling Price
  $2.5 million

Las Vegas' recently built Bellagio Hotel and Casino has garnered critical attention for its much-hyped fine-arts gallery. To complement the casino's artistic tendencies, Mikohn Lighting & sign fabricated this impression(istic)-able, double-faced, 200-foot-tall freestanding pylon, which incorporates an internally illuminated, flexible-face fabric display and a 12-foot-diameter, illuminated, flexible-face clock. The 16-foot-tall, halo-illuminated "Bellagio" letters are fabricated from steel.

The sign's computer-decorated faces, which measure 51 feet high by 65 feet wide, are supplied by Metromedia Technologies, Los Angeles. Mikohn's achievement is underscored by the project's quick turnaround time. The sign had to be designed, engineered, permitted and constructed in less than 120 days.

Fabricator
Young Electric Sign Co.
(YESCO)
Las Vegas
(702) 876-8080

Designers
Jim Gietzen
Helga Watkins
YESCO

Client
Rio Suite Hotel
and Casino

This 24 × 18-ft. metal and fiberglass structure surrounds the Rio kiosk at McCarren International Airport. The four-sided display was created to give a first impression upon the visitor's arrival. The open channel fronds, mask, crown and "Rio" copy are lined with double-tube neon. YESCO painted the fiberglass with high-gloss "candy" in multiple gradations and blends. The upper lamped raceways and four-tube open channel fingers burn steadily.

Fabricator
Shaw Sign & Awning Inc.
Fort Collins, CO
(970) 493-6244
Designer
Dallas Griffin
Shaw Sign & Awning Inc.

A little blue and red neon lighting go a long way to add a touch of water and sun to this subdivision sign. Fabricated, powder-coated aluminum letters, halo-lit with 4,500K neon, make up "Ridge West," while an internally mounted metal illumination barrier separates the sunset neon from the water neon. The display is set in a cultured stone wall.

Fabricator
Gordon Sign
Denver
(303) 629-6121
Designer
Ron Hull
Gordon Sign
Selling Price
$35,000

Measuring 49 feet high, this famous sunglass company's fabricated-aluminum sign is hard to miss. The 24 × 7-ft. aluminum cabinet features 2-inch flat retainers and semi-gloss black finish. Cooley Brite® eradicable flexible material is used on the backlit sign face, and 12 × 12-inch steel legs, painted semi-gloss white, are welded to the main support. Painted white with a light sand texture, the pole feet feature 12-inch returns around the supports. The bottom section of the sign is treated with anti-graffiti coating.

Existing Logo Signs: Mounted

Fabricator

Arrow Sign Co.
Oakland, CA
(510) 533-7693

Designers

Michael Manwaring
Tim Perks
The Office of Michael Manwaring
San Anselmo, CA
(415) 458-8100

Kevin Clinch
Ove Arup & Partners California
San Francisco
(415) 957-9445

Arrow Sign Co.

Client

Knight Ridder

This sign's 13-ft.-tall × 95-ft.-wide background comprises pre-finished aluminum composite material with a champagne-metallic finish that is bolted to a rolled steel frame with stainless-steel fasteners.

The structure's fabricated-aluminum letters feature acrylic faces and internal, fluorescent illumination. Supporting the sign is a 36-in.-wide steel flange beam fastened to the building with square tubing and pipe frame. A catwalk is located behind the sign's center for routine service.

Fabricator
  Neon Products Ltd.
  Vancouver, British Columbia
  (604) 215-5526
Designers
  John Peachey & Assoc.
  Vancouver
  (604) 984-4395

  Ed Pion
  Neon Products Ltd.
Client
  Oritalia

To create this restaurant's entrance sign, Neon Products incorporated three rolled aluminum panels with decorative shapes that are painted to resemble a blended antique finish. The middle panel is routed and backed with ivory plexiglas acrylic. Fluorescent lighting is installed behind the copy; additional lighting is housed in a box painted to match the structure.

Fabricator
Ad-Art Electronic Sign Corp.
Stockton, CA
(209) 931-0860

Designer
AAD Interiors-Architects
Scottsdale, AZ
(480) 998-4200

Client
Host Intl. Inc./Cinnabon

The dimensional 5-in.-deep, 15-ft., 4-in × 9-ft., 2-in. cup incorporates formed polycarbonate faces and a sculpted-foam handle that measures 5-ft., 7-in × 2-ft. Multi-colored designs and internal illumination with clear, red-neon squiggles are used to decorate the formed clear faces. The neon squiggles — constructed in four different depths and shapes — slowly flash on and off.

To create the "Cinnabon's" on the embossed sign panel, Ad-Art applied maroon and blue translucent film. Similiarly, sub-surface, white translucent film was used to create the panel's background. Constructed from three mirror-plex-surfaced "swirl" components, the "steam" is polished with clear aluminum. Chasing light-bulbs provide the aroma's illumination. The structure is supported by two steel tubes projecting from the wall.

Fabricator
National Sign
Seattle
(206) 282-0700

Designers
Chris Palmen
National Sign

GGLO
Seattle
(206) 467-5828

Client
Best Cellars

The 5 × 5-ft. logo sign, along with the 1 × 12-ft. copy, are routed out of aluminum panels and have a custom dark bronze patina textured finish. The copy is backed with white acrylic for maximum visibility. The logo was routed with no acrylic backing for an open feeling, and halo lit with concealed 6,500 white neon. The perimeter of the logo shape is lit with blue neon.

Fabricator
National Sign
Seattle
(206) 282-0700
Designer
Kay Rice
National Sign
Client
Wizards of the Coast

This mall logo sign is a layered, concave metal shape with routed push-through copy and graphics. The "Wizards" copy has custom painted purple vinyl laminated to the surface of the half-inch clear acrylic letters, allowing light to halo as well as illuminate the sign through the letter faces. The secondary copy has a custom color blend that has been painted on translucent clear vinyl and surface applied to the push-through letters. The acrylic starburst graphic was further pushed through from the copy to add more dimension.

The logo sign floats over another curved band that included "star" pinholes drilled into the aluminum face and backed with white acrylic and illuminated from behind. Underneath the curved sign band is another routed starburst and pinholes. The non-illuminated game pieces to the right of the sign are cut out of one-inch Sintra® with vinyl laminated to the surface. The backing panels are thin gauge Sintra® painted matte silver.

Fabricator
Planet Neon
Novi, MI
(248) 348-8150
Designer
Peterhansrea Design/JPRA
Farmington Hills, MI
(248) 737-0180

A 219-square-foot sign sums up this restaurant's appeal with air-brushed graphics of a pig and a sign cabinet shaped like a bone. The fabricated, wrap-around aluminum structure combines incandescent bulbs and pin-mounted reverse channel letters lit with neon.

Fabricator
  Arrow Sign Co.
  Oakland, CA
  (510) 533-7693
Designer
  Rick Cardinio
  Arrow Sign Co.
Client
  Dante's Restaurant

Arrow Sign created this restaurant signage with internally illuminated channel letters that were mounted onto a rolled-aluminum background, painted blue and decorated with vinyl. The yellow aluminum graphic was flat cut then mounted on pegs, as was the small white copy below the main text.

Fabricator
Federal Sign
Las Vegas
(702) 739-9466

Designer
Sue Deveny
Federal Sign

Client
Ghirardelli

This 25-ft, 9-in. × 6-ft., 6-in. marquee display was created in the fashion of the San Diego Gaslamp District while it was undergoing major renovations. Using an old black and white photo of the original marquee, and with strict guidelines from the Historical Preservation Committee, Federal Sign designed a marquee that they felt kept the basic integrity of the original design while creating a unique identity for their customer. The vast amount of various colored neon shaped in a Deco-design likeness was typical of the era.

Fabricator
Mikohn Lighting & Sign
Las Vegas
(702) 739-6789
Designers
Roger Pratt and
Jack W. Larsen Jr.
Mikohn Lighting & Sign
Selling Price
$2 million

The entrance, fabricated in the shape of a heart, blends 3-D molded fiberglass finished with high-gloss metal-flake gold and a cover channel with indirect ruby-red lighting.

The ribbon-shaped marquee, composed of 3-D fiberglass, is painted with a satin finish. The reverse-channel molded-fiberglass letters, finished in goldleaf, are brightened by a ruby-red halo.

Constructed of 3-D fiberglass and painted with a high-gloss finish to perfectly match the widely recognized yellow package, the M&M's bag serves as the sign's centerpiece. The candy's pan-channel logo letters stand 10 feet, 7 inches tall and are painted M&M brown. The letters, lit by 25-watt incandescent clear bulbs placed 6 inches on center, are accented by a single-stroke white neon outline. Animated grid neon simulates a shaking motion. The M&M pieces combine formed-plastic faces with internal neon illumination.

The supporting cast of M&M characters, painted high-gloss red, green and yellow, range in height from 15½ feet to 18 feet, 9 inches. They're constructed from 3-D fiberglass and are illuminated by directional flood lights.

Fabricator
Federal Sign
Las Vegas
(702) 739-9466
Designer
Sue Deveny
Federal Sign

To showcase its presence at the New York New York Hotel & Casino on the busy Las Vegas strip, the soft-drink giant Pepsi-Cola wanted a sign that would turn heads, yet fit in with the hotel's 1930s theme.

First, Federal Sign commissioned a mural featuring caricatures of '30s cops. Then, the company added a lamp-filled logo with a letter style typical of the era. The letters feature a variety of action sequences as well as a Bromo-Blue steady-burning neon outline. The bottle, illuminated with grid neon, slowly chases down to simulate soda emptying into the glass, which is also composed of grid neon. When the bottle is empty and the glass is full, Toki lights and fabricated ice cubes within the glass scintillate as bubbles rise to the top.

The policemen's hands extending from the mural are dimensionally sculpted from hard-coated foam. The message "Bigger Bottle — Better Flavor" contains exposed neon that flashes on and off.

Fabricator

International Sign & Design Corp.
Largo, FL
(727) 541-5573

Designers

International Sign & Design

Teller/Manok Architects
Laguna Beach, CA
(714) 497-7297

This House of Blues franchise wanted a sign that would convey the down-home flavor and rootsy nature of blues music. A rusted water tower provided a suitable framework. Affixed to this commanding structure is a double-faced aluminum cabinet measuring 4½ by 45 feet. It houses 2-foot, 8-inch channel letters highlighted with 15-millimeter Bromo-Blue neon, PK housings, and 12,000-volt transformers painted to appear aged. Crowning the tower are 3-foot, open-face aluminum channel letters fabricated with 15-millimeter Bromo-Blue neon, PK housings and 12,000-volt neon transformers.

Fabricators
Arrow Sign Co.
Oakland, CA
(510) 533-7693

OMC Industries
Bruan, TX
(800) 488-4662

Designers
Scott Bevan
Concept B
Concord, CA
(510) 682-8673

Dale Hoover
Hoover Assoc.
Bayfield, CO
(970) 884-0737

Addis Group
Berkely, CA
(510) 704-7500

Charlie Stroud
Arrow Sign Co.

Client
Ghirardelli Square

Ghirardelli Square is a San Francisco landmark in many ways. Domingo Ghirardelli set up shop in 1850, and his sons expanded the business, constructing a chocolate factory in 1893. When the plant became obsolete, a modern chocolate plant was built across the Bay. Later, a civic-minded San Franciscan bought the block to prevent demolition, asking that the renovation fuse both new and old red-brick factory buildings and preserve the famous electric sign, which was visible to ships entering the Bay. Although they couldn't preserve the aroma of the old chocolate works, designers created signage for the latest renovation of the shopping center that reflected the distinctive ambiance of the Municipal Pier area. The vertical directory features an extruded aluminum cabinet with white cove neon lighting. Decorated with rolled ¼-in. aluminum goldleaf letters, the supporting pipe is topped by a foam cone covered with a copper patina finish and a copper weathervane. Low-voltage fixtures mounted to the back of an I-beam provide flood lighting of the pedestal directory. Bronze and copper finishes unify the directories. Building identification signs feature aluminum backgrounds with flat, cut-out acrylic and aluminum fabricated elements. Directional signs are fabricated from cast bronze.

Fabricators
John Connor
Ian Hain
United Studios (USID)
Longwood, FL
(407) 831-3484

Designer
Walt Disney Imagineering
Longwood, FL
(407) 831-3484

Client
Walt Disney Imagineering

Selling Price
$82,050

The 11 × 12-ft., 8-in. entry kiosk to Walt Disney Imagineering theme park is constructed of an aluminum frame with a stainless-steel background overlay, distressed using a hand-grinder and then clearcoated. End-radiused elements are fabricated from aluminum with a tarnished brass faux finish, and pearlized Nova colors decorate the Lexan globes. On the circular dimensional sign, 1-in. deep, waterjet-cut acrylic copy protrudes through the stainless-steel background panel. Illumination on this display is 15mm neon tubing in various colors. The center medallion "light bulb" consists of white neon tubing fabricated in a grid format to provide illumination behind the Dura Trans face. The four sectional portions of the display consist of alternate colors that include 15mm orange, pink, purple and blue. The Kodak® copy is backlit with fluorescent lighting.

Fabricators
Paul Tyree
Ian Hain
United Studios (USID)
Longwood, FL
(407) 831-3484

Designer
Walt Disney Imagineering
Longwood, FL
(407) 831-3484

Client
Walt Disney Imagineering

Selling Price
$56,470

Fabricated from stainless steel with an internally illuminated ABC cabinet incorporating routed/push-through copy, the marquee features 6-ft. tall, hand-sculpted dimensional foam letters with ¼-in.-plate aluminum characters in front of them. The ABC Sound Studio sign mounted on a 70-ft. antenna structure is fabricated from two stainless steel circles with exposed neon in multi-level letter-sets and arrows. The "Radio Disney" sign comprises individual illuminated channel letters and hand-sculpted, 3-in.-deep foam letters finished in high-gloss enamel. A secondary marquee illustrates ¼-in. thick "Doug" characters and copy cutouts with re-furbished aluminum TV sets from another display. All illumination in the ABC cabinets and television-set graphics use 15mm 6500 white neon tubing, while the "Radio Disney" channel letters incorporate 15mm clear red neon tubing.

Fabricator
Gary Stemler
Nordquist Sign Co.
Minneapolis, MN
(612) 823-7291
Designer
Jack Rouse Assoc.
Cincinnati, OH
(513) 381-0055
Client
Kellogg's Cereal City
Selling Price
$200,000

Nordquist Sign Co. custom fabricated this entertainment industry graphic using a quarter-inch aluminum plate to create some logo dimension. The letters are ⅛-in. aluminum in six-in. returns, giving an overall size of 30 × 80-ft. The collage is also created with fabricated aluminum panels covered with 3M Scotchprint® graphics and vinyl detail.

Fabricator
Bill Buttram
YESCO (Interior Sign Branch)
Young Electric Sign Co.
Las Vegas, NV
(702) 876-8080

Designers
Helga Watkins
Jim Lietzen
YESCO

Client
Mandalay Bay Resort & Casino

This variety of handcarved, sculpted and cast elements utilizes substrates from MDO board, Sign•Foam®, fiberglass resin, tin and sheet metal.

Fabricator
Bill Buttram
YESCO (Interior Sign Branch)
Young Electric Sign Co.
Las Vegas, NV
(702) 876-8080

Designers
Helga Watkins
Chris Mohan
Junior Hapitana
Mike Bednash
YESCO

Client
Venetian Resort Hotel Casino

Like other Young Electric Sign projects, each sign is an original design. The signs are a mix of materials and manufacturing techniques used to achieve the old look of Venice in a casino environment.

Fabricator
Designage Inc.
Apopka, FL
(407) 884-6600

Designers
Designage Inc.

Joe Drivas Photography
Longwood, FL
(407) 321-1969

Designed to guide guests through the new 16,000-square-foot Information Center at Florida's Kennedy Space Center, this sign system blasts off with an 8 × 54-foot halo that combines a Durst Lambda photoprint and blue neon. Five 3 × 10-foot oval, illuminated, routed signs with push-through graphics and Chemetal® swirled aluminum decorate the faces. To allow flexibility in relocating or adding new signs, cabinets are mounted to a five-row aluminum pipe raceway. The 8 × 8-foot, free-standing "Shuttle Status" wall consists of two Prolite® LED displays, which track upcoming launches and landings.

Finally, the "Space Shop" sign is fabricated with cut-out acrylic letters mounted to a sculpted, high-density foam, perforated-aluminum panel, stainless-steel bars and a mounting plate.

Fabricator
Superior Electrical Adv. Inc.
Long Beach, CA
(562) 495-3808

Designer
Joe Marks
Superior Electrical Adv. Inc.

Created for a skatepark in Orange, CA, this system's main display fascia, built from galvanized steel panels and wire mesh, resembles a slightly deconstructed skateboard ramp. The Vans logo and letters feature aluminum channel construction with white acrylic faces and blue vinyl overlays. Blue and white neon illuminate the interior. Individual skater figures, pegged 4 inches off the wall, are flat, cut-out aluminum painted with Superior's pewter finish. Blue neon silhouettes the skaters with a halo glow. The Vans Shoes sign, composed of a single-faced cabinet with brushed-aluminum faces, features routed, push-through acrylic letters with translucent-red overlay lit by interior fluorescent light.

Fabricator
International Sign & Design Corp.
Largo, FL
(727) 541-5573

Designers
Greteman Group
Wichita, KS
(316) 263-1007

Law/Kingdom Inc.
Wichita
(316) 268-0230

Three 12 × 25-foot, internally illuminated monument signs anchor the system for this shopping center. The main text is routed out and pushed through with ½-inch plexiglas acrylic. The aluminum dome, decorated with routed-out stars and slashes backed with plex, is marked with an "H" composed of two vertical aluminum tubes crossed with a routed-out strip and star. The dome is housed in an all-steel frame and .125 aluminum skin.

Each main entrance sign features internal illumination, measures 13 feet in diameter and is composed of steel and encased in fiberglass. All the circles on both the front and back are routed out and backed with plexiglas acrylic. A single stroke of purple neon highlights the dome on the front and back.

Fabricator
Luminous Neon Inc.
Hutchinson, KS
(316) 662-2363

Designer
Gardner Design
Wichita, KS
(316) 691-8808

Selling Price
$23,558

Created to add an authentic flavor to a steakhouse, these displays identify the restaurant's interior service areas. The silhouettes of pots and pans, complete with plumes of steam, are flat, cut-out aluminum backlit with clear red neon. The creamery display, marked by aluminum open-channel letters featuring exposed neon, incorporates two stainless-steel milk jugs, two three-legged milking stools, six antique milk bottles, livestock bells, turned wooden spindles, wood bric-a-brac, an ice cream churn, a wooden table and a bent sheet-metal fan.

To authenticate the bakery display, designers added antique-metal pie pans, glass mason jars that contain flickering light bulbs, a wooden barrel, bundt cake pans, tart pans and such kitchen staples as a ceramic crock and bowl, a hand crank mixer and a metal whisk.

Finally, the grill display, featuring exposed neon and backlit neon behind the stars, yokes together a rectangular aluminum tube frame with five plow disks, three sets of bull horns with leather and wood mountings, steel windmill blades, and barbed wire.

Fabricators
Signs Etc.
Lexington, KY
(606) 276-3646

Bush Builders
Sevierville, TN
(865) 453-8376

Designer
Brother Zank
Custom Craftsman Signs
Sevierville, TN
(865) 429-1934

Client
Citizens National Bank

Stability and permanence are combined with this automated moving-message display. The 15-ft. internally-illuminated HID, embossed-face sign incorporates softly illuminated upper roof window units. Brother Zank used a simple brick base and a 5-watt, wedge-base Time-O-Matic incandescent message center. Custom Craftsman Signs finished the sign with a landscaping redesign and a plant bed.

Fabricator
Ad-Art Electronic Sign Corp.
Stockton, CA
(209) 931-0860
Designer
Jack DuBois
Ad-Art Electronic Sign Corp.

Designed for a Daly City, CA, shopping center, this 60-foot-tall, double-faced pylon features what is being billed as the first high-resolution, full-color LED video display of its type in California. The fabricated-metal, 23-foot, 8-inch-wide pylon incorporates 3 × 2-foot, 2-inch open-channel letters, which are finished with teal and illuminated with double-tube green neon. The 10-inch "center" letters combine teal paint and green neon. The twin horizontal "rule lines" above and below are brightened by magenta paint and illuminated with rose neon tubing.

The fabricated-metal background is finished in Dunn-Edwards Cottage White. Removable, continuous fiberglass shells cap the vertical edges of the pylon. The sign's fabricated, metal-recessed central panel features an arch opening and a teal sand-stucco finish. Trim detail accents trace the arch's profile, mimicking the shopping center's existing arched entryway. These recessed, teal-colored surfaces glow with halo light emanating from concealed, 3,500 white neon.

The sign's most eye-catching component, the double-faced, 12 × 16-foot LED, boasts a 144 × 192-pixel matrix, which produces more than 16.7 million color possibilities and provides full-video capability.

Fabricator
Nordquist Sign Co.
Minneapolis
(612) 823-7291
Designer
R.J. Heisenbottle
Coral Gables, FL
(305) 446-7799
Client
Gusman Center for the
Performing Arts
Selling Price
$120,000

You can't miss a show with a digital display like this. The theater marquee was fabricated from aluminum cabinets mounted to a steel substructure. The "Olympia" text is illuminated with marquee lamps. This sign also incorporates electronic message centers on three sides.

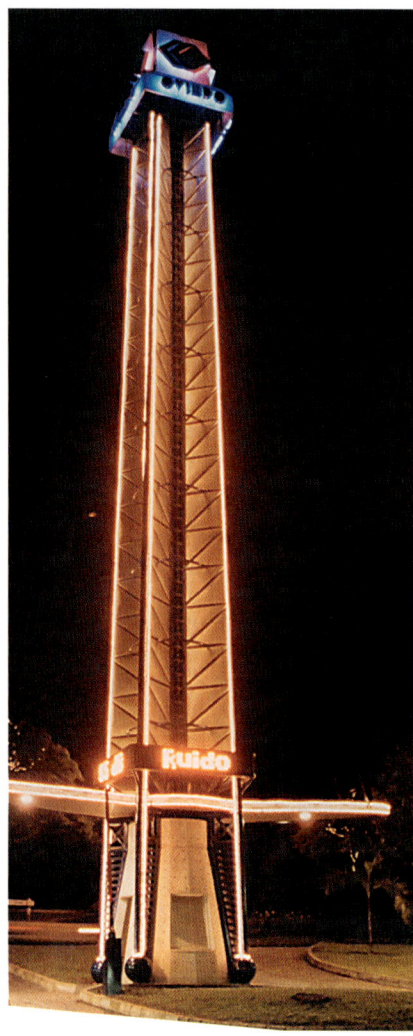

Fabricator and Designer
Vaitronik S. A.
Pereira, Risoralda, Colombia
+57(96) 337-7500
Client
Centro Comercial Oviedo

This 528-lb. landmark has a 759-ft. viewing distance. Colombia-based Vaitronik used a square-tubing frame covered by sheet metal, 1,484 aluminum reflectors and a electronic display comprising of 27 power control cards for a well-lit, modular version of the Eiffel Tower. Hardly the usual time-and-temperature sign, the LED display shows other environmental conditions such as carbon monoxide, relative humidity and noise level.

Fabricators
Custom Craftsman Signs
Sevierville, TN
(865) 429-1934

Joseph Construction Co.
Sevierville, TN
(865) 428-7900

Designer
Brother Zank
Custom Craftsman Signs

Client
Citizens National Bank

This 15-ft. stone and stucco monument includes a steel frame work and cultured stone. The logo faces are a unique edge-lit "plug-in system" which uses thick acrylic and aluminum bars. Other features include cast aluminum name letters, a Time-O-Matic, 5-watt wedge base message center, landscaping, curbwork and bolder design.

Fabricator
Mikohn Lighting & Sign
Las Vegas
(702) 739-6789
Designer
Jack M. Larsen Jr.
Mikohn Lighting & Sign
Selling Price
$4 million

In most deserts, mirages lure travelers with visions of swaying palm trees, fresh water and undulating belly dancers. But in Las Vegas, the mirages are made of neon and massive digital displays that promote headliners like stand-up comedian Jackie Mason. The Sahara Hotel & Casino shelled out big bucks for this MikohnVision electronic board. Measuring 30 feet high and 48 feet wide, the EMC features a full-color, 224 × 376 pixel matrix.

Above the message board, 15-foot-tall camels support a texcote-finished castle crowned by a high-gloss gold minaret.

Fabricator
    Ad-Art Electronic Sign Corp.
    Stockton, CA
    (209) 931-0860
Designers
    William Budnik
    Tony Ortega
    Ad-Art Electronic Sign Corp.
Client
    Crystal Church

The 17-ft., 2-in. × 26-ft., 10-in. monument display for a famous television worship center utilizes an Ad-Art full-color LED display. The monument is fabricated aluminum construction with a white sand-textured finish. The beveled edges and returns are surfaced with .040 polished clear aluminum, as is the border trim, acting as a retainer, surrounding the black LED display. The 12-in. "Crystal Cathedral" copy is R/O with half-inch clear acrylic push-through letters that are surfaced with polished clear aluminum and internally illuminated for a halo effect.

Fabricator
Federal Sign
Las Vegas
(702) 739-9466
Designer
Sue Deveny
Federal Sign

When the operators of the Santa Fe Hotel & Casino contracted with Federal Sign, their goal was two-fold. First, they wanted to replace an existing pylon sign while still retaining the pipes and footings. They also wanted a colorful focal point to draw traffic from a nearby freeway exit. Federal responded by creating a top cabinet to reflect the casino's logo, which was inspired by Native American headdresses. The lamp-filled letters are bolstered by a steady-burning Voltarc purple-neon outline. Designer Sue Deveny continued the feather effect down the cabinet's side to frame the full-color 24 × 30-foot, wedge-based electronic message center. Standing 80 feet tall and 49 feet wide, the sign commands the landscape and beckons travelers to blaze a trail to the Santa Fe.

Fabricator
Ad-Art Electronic Sign Corp.
Stockton, CA
(209) 931-0860
Designers
Charles F. Barnard, Betty Willis,
William Hannapple and Dave Schultz
Ad-Art Electronic Sign Corp.

Created to mark the multi-million dollar expansion of the Las Vegas Convention Center, this digital display pairs state-of-the-art LED technology with a touch of nostalgia. The 45-foot-high, three-sided pylon display harks back to an internationally recognized 1958 sign.

This homage is particularly evident in the three radiused, diamond sign panels containing 4-foot, 4-inch to 2-foot open channel letters in "lipstick script" that spell out "Las Vegas." These letters are surfaced with purple acrylic mirror and illuminated with computer-driven Tecnolux #14 magenta neon. The metal, reverse-channel "Convention Center" letters are painted bright magenta, pegged off the background and halo illuminated with D/T 30 MA white neon. The 8-foot-wide border consists of D/T coral-rose neon with 7C7 clear, scintillating lamps between the channels.

Topping the sign is a fabricated eight-point star, painted bright magenta with red returns. It is illuminated with a ruby-red neon outline and tip-to-tip clear-red neon centers, and showcases clear scintillating lamps at the center.

The three 11 × 20-foot LED displays, boasting full-color, full-motion video, are housed in three-sided fabricated-metal cabinets with radius ends.

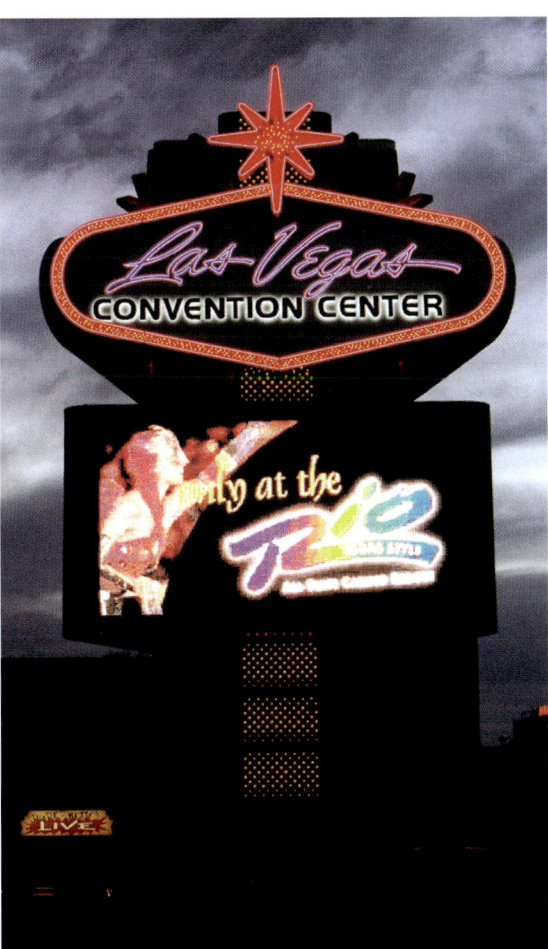

Exposed Neon

Fabricator
  Superior Electrical Adv. Inc.
  Long Beach, CA
  (562) 495-3808
Designer
  Miguel Rieman
  Superior Electrical Adv. Inc.

Produced for an Aliso Viejo, CA-based cinema, this interior, exposed-neon sign features aluminum panels with curved neon accents. The letters in "Edwards" incorporate aluminum, Alliance metal and exposed, double-tube, clear red neon. These letters are installed on a curved, aluminum, tube-like structure. Dimmer lighting is used on the theater's lower levels.

Fabricator
Neon Products Ltd., a Div. of
the Jim Pattison Group
Richmond, British Columbia
(604) 274-5584

Designer
Dennis Caulder
Neon Products

The plans for "Java Hut" entailed installing two, single-faced, illuminated displays on an existing projecting framework. "The" is made from S.T. gold neon, and the 2-foot "Java Hut" open-channel letters are illuminated with S.T. red neon. Measuring 6-feet tall, the sheet-metal palm tree incorporates PMS green and yellow paint and S.T. green and gold neon. "Bakery & Café" is made from 3M cardinal-red vinyl, flush letters and a single, red-neon tube. PMS blue and beige paint and medium-blue neon make up the sign's background. The sign measures 17 feet by 6 inches.

Fabricator
　Neon-Line Werbedesign GES. M.B.H.
　Vienna, Austria
　+43 (1) 332-0607

Designers
　Dusty Sprengnagel and Nicki Schreinlechner
　Neon-Line Werbedesign

The term "Bora" refers to a cold, northerly wind of the Adriatic. However, there's nothing chilly about a bar and café that serves warm drinks and spirits. This double-faced sign is mounted on an aluminum case with a vinyl background to create daytime visibility. Pyrex® neon tubing is used to illuminate the sign. Photos by Dusty Sprengnagel.

Fabricators
Ad-Art Electronic Sign Corp.
Stockton, CA
(209) 931-0860

Alert-Lite
Sun Valley, CA
(818) 767-2059

Designers
Charles Barnard
Ad-Art Electronic Sign Corp.

John Gaby
Historic Resources Group
Hollywood, CA
(323) 469-2349

Client
American Cinematheque

Restoration of the Egyptian Theater, Hollywood, involved re-creating its original neon-blade skin. The 32-ft., 6-in. × 4-ft., 9-in. double-faced display was designed from '20s and '30s archival photos and data provided by the Historical Resources Group. The sign faces are ⅛-in.-thick aluminum plate with a single-hairline butt seam behind the top of the letter "T." Low-luster ICI Dulux™ acrylic satin-paint finishes that match ICI Dulux enamels used throughout include special color formulations of cobalt, bright gold, dark burnished gold, dark mauve-blue, earthtone red, turquoise and white. To replicate original glass-work and "period-style" stand-offs, Alert-Lite used either the original neon or the nearest contemporary match. Tube colors are cobalt clear (argon/mercury); clear novial gold (helium); novial green-clear (argon/mercury); ruby clear; cobalt clear (neon); and clear blue (argon/mercury). The 2-ft, 4-in. letters are fabricated MTL-raised block construction with white faces and outlined with clear red neon.

The supporting ironwork for the projecting sign simulates the original support structure. Neon animation is provided by a three-position, two-point flasher that controls the decorative neon "lattices" on each edge of the sign.

Fabricator
Kiss Graphics Pty. Ltd.
Gold Coast, Queensland, Australia
+61 (7) 5593-7611
Designers
Greg Graham and Alexander Kiss
Kiss Graphics
Selling Price
$10,500 (Australian)

If you're seeking the perfect gaming venue, you might try placing your bets at this Queensland-based hotel and casino. The 7-by-6-by-1-foot, exposed-neon sign features an aluminum enclosure with a black-painted face. The lettering and dance-hall girl are made from bent, 9-millimeter, ruby-red, novial-gold, orange, peach, pink and brilliant-blue Masonlite neon. All neon tubing is mounted on the black aluminum face in layers. Finishing touches include the sign's clear-acrylic face and gold-laminated frame.

Fabricator
Neon-Line Werbedesign
GES. M.B.H.
Vienna, Austria
(43) 1-332-0607
Designers
Dusty Sprengnagel
Nicki Schreinlechner
(Graphic-Lettering)
Neon-Line Werbedesign
Client
Hannes Boslinc
GES. M.B.H.

Varnished aluminum channel letters have an opal acrylic front that includes a "steaming"digital photoprint. The lower sign is backlit with warm white neon tubes and outlined with orange neon. Photo by Dusty Sprengnagel.

Fabricator
Federal Sign (Arlington Plant)
Las Vegas, NV
(702) 739-9466
Designer
Sue Deveny
Federal Sign
Client
Ghirardelli, Las Vegas

Identifing the Ghirardelli shop at Harrah's Hotel & Casino on the Las Vegas Strip, this 22 × 9-ft. double-faced sign could attract the most avid dieter. The 18-in. lamp-filled letters flash with a steadily burning novial-gold neon border. A clear, red neon grid chases down the sides as the lamped border chases clockwise. The ice-cream graphics are computer airbrushed using CorelDRAW!™ 8 and CorelPhoto-Paint™ on vinyl and highlighted with multicolored constant neon outlines and a flashing cherry. The almond chips are scintillating Toki lights

Fabricator
Jeff King
Frisbie Sign Co.
Alto, MI
(616) 868-0092
Designers
Jim Frisbie
Jeff King
Frisbie Sign Co.
Client
Medieval Day "Castle"
Selling Price
$7,500

This glowing dragon, made of EGL and Technolux neon, soars through a medieval castle. Before the dragon could breathe fire, however, it had to be filled with neon and argon, fitted together with GTO wire, blocked out with black aqua blockout paint and finished with aluminum, EGL electrodes and electrical-rated plastic.

Fabricator
Ad-Art Electronic Sign Corp.
Stockton, CA
(209) 931-0860

Designer
Godfredsen-Sigal Architects
Venice, CA
(310) 664-0302

Client
Hustler Video

A 10-ft diameter, illuminated rotating open-grid world dominates this Sunset Blvd. video store in Hollywood. The globe grid is rolled and welded 2 × 2-ft. square aluminum tubing, painted silver. The world "continents" are formed Lexan® that is painted silver and outlined with white neon. 18-in. self-contained metal channel letters were painted red and illuminated with clear red neon. The globe's copy wrap reads "For the Rest of the World." The globe revolves on top a 27-ft, 7-in.-high spindle element — a rolled, brushed aluminum, tapered cover that conceals a supporting I-beam. Thirteen rings of multi-colored neon chase from bottom to top. A 3-ft, 10-in. sign band on a 14-ft. radius wraps the entrance canopy. The face and returns are brushed aluminum with narrow shields on the top and bottom, concealing white neon accents. Two sets of 2-ft., 2-in. "Hustler" letters, inset, painted red and illuminated with clear red neon, are installed on the curved face of the band. Underneath, 9-in. open channel letters are suspended under the canopy and illuminated with white neon. Additional signwork is distributed across two building elevations.

Fabricator
Neon-Line Werbedesign GES. M.B.H.
Vienna, Austria
(43) 1-332-0607
Designer
Dusty Sprengnagel
Neon-Line Werbedesign GES. M.B.H.
Client
1516 Brewing Co.

Photo by Dusty Sprengnagel.

Exposed Neon

Fabricator
 Ultraneon Sign Co.
 San Diego
 (619) 569-6716
Designer
 David Green
 Ultraneon Sign Co.
Selling Price
 $45,000

"Sporting" a look of its own, this exposed-neon display calls a heavily signed outdoor mall its home. The 15-foot-tall, aluminum, wall-mounted players are cut to shape and covered with digitally printed vinyl graphics. Mounted on an existing awning, the "Just Sports" logo incorporates halo and face illumination and is flanked by a ¼-inch aluminum rod. White neon is used to outline the sports fans.

Fabricator
National Sign
Seattle
(206) 282-0700
Designer
Ken Krumpos
National Sign
Client
Downtown Self Storage

This 3 × 18-ft. double-faced neon illuminated display is made from painted fabricated aluminum extrusion. The graphic
on top is cut out of aluminum with neon
outlines. The "Downtown" copy is horizontal blue neon surrounded by horizontal purple neon and two vertical clear red
stripes. The "Self Storage" 3-ft. 6-in. ×
10-ft. V-shaped cabinet includes
exposed clear red and 6,500 white neon
illumination.

Fabricator
Cindy Parrish
Ram Sign Studios
Farmington, NM
(505) 326-5801
Designer
Cindy Parrish

Ram Sign Studios constructed this 3 × 3-ft. pyramid-shaped sculpture with ½-in. wood sides covered with red, green and blue laminant. Each side is accented by a 15mm classic colored neon tube that follows the contour of the arch at the bottom edge. The neon tubes are finished at the end with a euro-style "butt-welding" technique. The sculpture stands on three 4-in. black painted wood balls and is topped by a black bowling ball. This is twice encircled by a 15mm classic golden yellow neon tube with bubbles blown randomly along its length. The neon flow-scripting transporter is mounted inside the body so that only the power cord is visible.

Fabricator
Neon-Line Werbedesign
GES M.B.H.
Vienna, Austria
+43 (1) 332-0607
Designer
Dusty Sprengnagel
Neon-Line Werbedesign

This "floating" neon display was installed to celebrate a Vienna, Austria-based film festival. Blue Pyrex® neon tubing and red-colored glass are used to create the V'iennale logo. "Gartenbau Kino" remains a permanent part of the cinema's outdoor signage. Photo by Dusty Sprengnagel.

Fabricator
Ross Waldberg
Art After Dark
Thousand Oaks, CA
(805) 493-1688
Designer
Ross Waldberg
Art After Dark
Selling Price
$1,250

The 16 × 13 × 6-in. glass for this table is sand-blast carved with paint applied to carved glass areas, multiple colors by DEKA and 1Shot paints. The frosted glass edge has scalloped-edge effects. The base has gray granite laminate applied to wood. Clear gold tubing with pumped mercury argon is inside the base, lighting the glass design.

Fabricator
Fedele Musso
Ultra Neon
Jupiter, FL
(561) 744-1833
Designer
Fedele Musso
Ultra Neon
Client
Royal Grille at the
Port Royal Hotel
Selling Price
$2,000

For this hotel decoration, backlit neon fixtures were fabricated from brushed aluminum and highlighted with glass jewels and stained birch along a 15-ft. curved wall to concur with retro modernism design. All major glass manufacturers, EGL, Voltare, FMS and Accuwall, were used to achieve the color effects desired, particularly the classic glass in between the fixtures, which shed more subdued light to eliminate glare.

Multi-Tenant/Main ID Signs

Fabricator
National Sign
Seattle
(206) 282-0700

Designer
Ken Krumpos
National Sign

Client
208th St. Station

The texture and color of the 208th St. Station tenant sign make it stand out from the crowd. The fabricated acrylic numerals are painted opaque black with a white outline, allowing for a halo effect behind the letters and illuminating the letter faces themselves. The wordboxes consist of channel wraps with painted acrylic graphics. A gold neon oval contrasts with the purple halo behind the galvanized corrugated background. The tenant displays are made from Signpac™ extruded aluminum with surface-applied graphics.

Fabricator
Don Bell Industries Inc.
Port Orange, FL
(904) 788-8084
Designer
Development Design Group Inc.
Baltimore
(410) 962-0505
Client
Muvico Theaters/Paradise 24 Entertainment Park
Selling Price
$90,000

"This side of Paradise," a 50 × 38-ft. multi-tenant pylon sign, identifies Muvico Theater's entertainment park and cinemas. The aluminum-clad structure uses colors and motifs from the time when everyone walked like an Egyptian. The sign also features 3-ft.-wide × 9-in.-tall, acrylic-faced channel lettters; an internally illuminated, acrylic, graphic panel; and a sign cabinet for use by six future tenants.

Fabricator
Claude Neon, a division of
Jim Pattison Sign Group
Dorval, Quebec
(514) 856-7756
Designers
Louise Bouré (architect)

Stephane Dusablon
Claude Neon
Client
Place St. Eustache
Selling Price
$30,000 (Canadian)

The upper portion of the Place St. Eustache tenant sign is fabricated from aluminum and paint, and incorporates ½-in.-deep, PVC cut letters. Indirect illumination is provided by halogen fixtures, while the tenants section is made from aluminum extrusion with individual, vinyl-covered, white plastic faces. Direct illumination is provided by HO floor lamps; the décor is fabricated from painted aluminum. The entire sign measures 18 ft., 9 in. × 36 ft.

Fabricator
Arrow Sign Co.
Oakland, CA
(510) 533-7693
Designer
Charlie Stroud
Arrow Sign Co.
Client
Ravenswood 101

Each Ravenswood 101 tenant sign's aluminum letters incorporates an exposed-neon outline. Supported by texture-finish pipes, the structures also feature aluminum end caps with exposed neon, while each flexible and rigid sign face is illuminated with internal fluorescent fixtures. The two Ravenswood signs measure 65 ft. tall and incorporate angle iron trusses.

Multi-Tenant/Main ID Signs

Fabricator
Superior Sign Systems
Vacaville, CA
(707) 449-8111
Designer
Sid Aslami
Superior Sign Systems
Selling Price
$510,000

To create the 29 × 55-foot double-sided pylons and the 20 × 32-foot four-sided pylon shown here, Superior Sign Systems employed three primary ingredients: .125 aluminum, McNichols' perforated .125 aluminum and Wrisco's black-anodized aluminum. The pan-channel letters in "Bridgepointe" contain 3/16-inch yellow, Acrylite acrylic faces mounted on an illuminated, curved, perforated panel. The perforated panel is backed with black/white acrylic and illuminated with H.O. fluorescent tubing. Steel tubes — measuring 2 × 8 inches with 1½ × 4-inch, steel-channel overlays — are used to produce the horizontal bars between the tenant panels.

Fabricator
Don Bell Industries Inc.
Port Orange, FL
(904) 788-8084

Designer
Development Design Group Inc.
Baltimore
(410) 962-0505

Client
Muvico Theaters/Pompano 18

Selling Price
$45,000

The pylon entry identification sign for Muvico Theater's Pompano Beach 18 screen cinema follows the theme of a 1950's drive-in. The "retro" pylon sign is inspired by motel signs found alongside the American roadside. The 30 ×16 ft., aluminum-clad sign features open channel letters with exposed neon, acrylic-faced sign boxes with applied vinyl and small twinkling lights.

Multi-Tenant/Main ID Signs

Fabricator
Ultraneon Sign Co.
San Diego
(619) 569-6716
Designer
Westfield Design & Construction
Los Angeles
(310) 478-4456
Selling Price
$38,000

Standing 30 feet tall, this multi-tenant pylon contains an aluminum construction with an STO finish. Translucent vinyl copy makes up the sign's cabinet, while ¾-inch, clear-acrylic, push-through letters make up the structure's identification text. The 5-foot, 4-inch, round-logo, open-pan channel letters feature corrugated metal and exposed neon.

Fabricator
YESCO
Denver
(303) 375-9933
Designer
J.D. Easton
YESCO
Selling Price
$42,000

Check out City Center's 9-foot, 6-inch-by-14-foot cabinet display. The main-ID sign incorporates aluminum and yellow paint. Routed, ½-inch, acrylic push-through letters covered with first-surface translucent orange vinyl are used to create "City Center." The "Marketplace" letters are 3-inch-deep, reverse-channel letters that are painted blue and peg-mounted 1 inch from the cabinet. Fluorescent lamps are used to internally illuminate the entire cabinet. Off Shot blue paint and two, 15-millimeter, exposed, ultra-blue neon tubes make up the sign's "upper wave."

Fabricator
Superior Sign Systems
Vacaville, CA
(707) 449-8111
Designers
Komorous-Towey Architects
San Francisco
(415) 522-6622

Sid Aslami
Superior Sign Systems
Selling Price
$140,000

Eight-by-8-inch steel uprights and 2-by-4-inch, steel-tube horizontal and cross bars support this pylon that greets visitors of the Sierra Vista shopping center. The structure also employs a .125 aluminum pole and a base cover, as well as two 7-by-7-foot internally illuminated, Lexan®-faced cabinets. 3M's opaque, antique-white vinyl is used to cover the Lexan faces; 3M's translucent vinyl is used to create "Sierra Vista." A matching steel roof crowns the structure.

The commercial sign industry has been affected by the same technological advances as the electric side. Specifically, images output directly to computer-cut vinyl have decreased the time required executing a design, thereby creating a new niche within the industry of "fast signs" offering one-day or same-day delivery. Practically every commercial signshop offers vinyl lettering or more, and many have begun to incorporate the photo-realistic advantage of digital imaging on vinyl with more traditional methods of painting, carving and gilding signs. Often traditional methods, including sandblasting, are applied to new materials, such as high-density urethane. Many of today's well-designed and fabricated signs involve a combination of materials and techniques. While there is no denying the emergence of vinyl in commercial signmaking, traditional techniques will always be necessary to create unique signs.

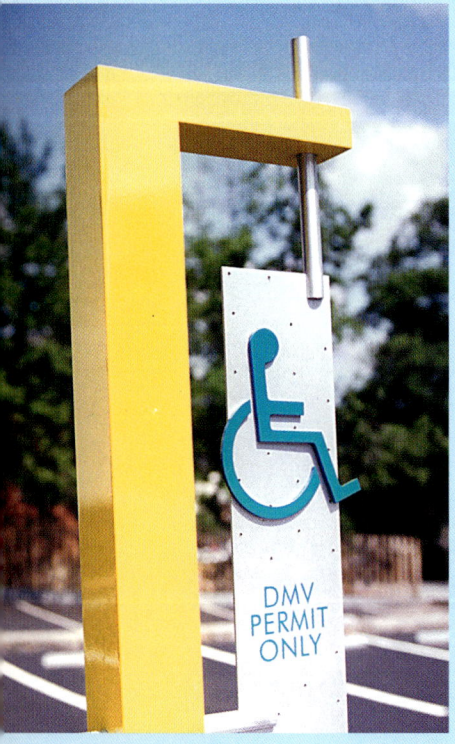

Fabricator
MSI
Corona, CA
(909) 734-3970

Designer
Clare Conner
MSI
Portland, OR
(503) 239-7398

Client
Lennar

Selling Price
$6,462

The face of this 5-ft., 6-in. × 30-in. faux stone sign is designed using painted copy, exterior-grade photo vinyl logo art. The sign is finished with a natural-finished wood post, copper cap and wrought iron frame and details. The project was designed and illustrated using a Macintosh™ and Adobe Illustrator©.

Fabricator
  Natural Graphics Inc.
  Houston
  (713) 661-5075
Designer
  Katie Hatch
  Natural Graphics Inc.
Client
  Callaway Development Corp.
Selling Price
  $3,698

This 12 × 8-ft. freestanding sign was designed to evoke the feeling of a musical instrument. The sign was constructed using painted Gerber vinyl applied to Duraply™ plywood, accented with redwood. The M-scroll and details were airbrushed.

Fabricator
Al Bolek
Sign Concepts
Addison, IL
(630) 495-7446

Designers
Al and Lynda Bolek
Sign Concepts

Client
Lalo's Mexican Restaurant

Selling Price
$775

This 4 × 8½-ft. MDO restaurant sign was airbrushed and roller-blended using 1Shot lettering enamels. The background was two-color, sponge-painted in shades of turquoise.

Fabricator
Sign Design
Wooster, OH
(330) 262-8838

Designer
Ken Stiffler
Sign Design

Client
Jim Moser Auto Sales

Selling Price
$1,630

This 4-ft. × 8-ft., 6-in. MDO signboard features computer-cut vinyl letters (including the prismatic effect) and a 1Shot enamel background.

Flat Signs: Freestanding

Fabricator
 Graphic Services Inc.
 Manassas, VA
 (703) 368-5578
Designer
 Gary Godby
 Graphic Services Inc.
Client
 Jones-Miller House

This double-faced, MDO-backed sign measures 36 × 54 in., with a ¾-in. wood frame. The ribbon is cut out of ½-in. MDO and airbrushed with 1Shot enamels. "The Jones-Miller House" copy is cut-out plex letters, gilded with 23K gold leaf. The border and accents are also 23K gold. The plaques are comprised of cut-out MDO with vinyl lettering, masked and sprayed graphics in 1Shot enamel.

Fabricator
  Tullochgorum Signs
  Ormstown, Quebec
  (450) 829-3933
Designer
  Loraine Lamb Lalonde
  Tullochgorum Signs
Client
  Ilsa Laliberté

This 30 × 20-in., double-sided MDO sign was designed using Gerber Graphix Advantage® software, and painted with 1Shot enamels, using Gerber mask stencil. The panel edges were prefinished with West-System epoxy. It was installed on the client's existing post.

Fabricator
Bunting Graphics Inc.
Verona, PA
(412) 820-2200
Designers
W. Todd Vaught and
Michael Neiswander
Sky Design
Atlanta, GA
(404) 688-4702
Client
Fletcher Martin
Selling Price
$3,600

Paralleling exterior signage with interior design for greater recognizability, the makers of this 4½ × 9-ft. × ⅛-in. identification sign matched the curved lines of the bottom plate to interior curved planning. The signmakers used brushed aluminum routed to expose paint beneath.

Fabricator
   Tullochgorum Signs
   Ormstown, Quebec
   (450) 829-3933
Designer
   Loraine Lamb Lalonde
   Tullochgorum Signs
Client
   Ferme Biologique Burtonville

This 46 × 50 × ¾-in. MDO sign hangs on the barn of an organic meat farm. Painting the sign entirely with lettering enamels, the artist used Gerber GRAPHIX ADVANTAGE® software for the design. The cow and calf illustration is hand-rendered.

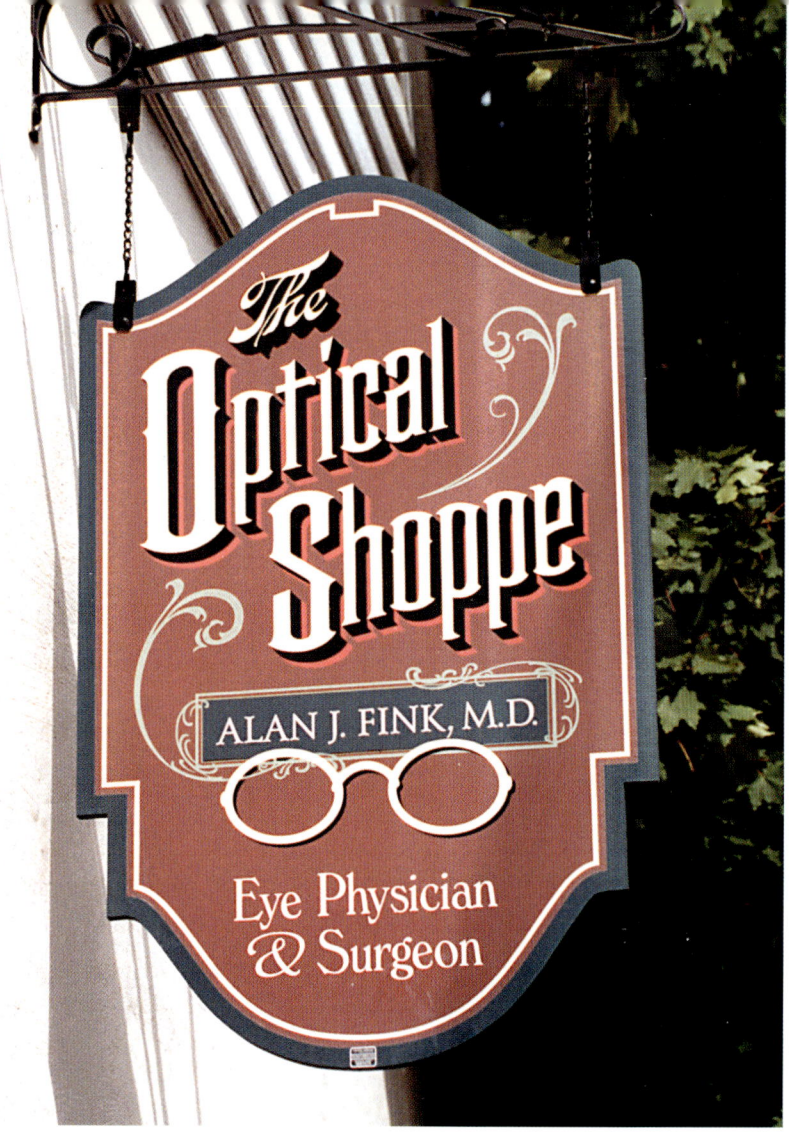

Fabricator
Graphic Services Inc.
Manassas, VA
(703) 368-5578
Designer
Gary Godby
Graphic Services Inc.
Client
The Optical Shoppe

This hanging sign measures 28 × 42 in., and is constructed of ¾-in. MDO with vinyl lettering and accents. "The Optical Shoppe" copy is printed by a GerberEDGE®. The border and background are painted with bulletin enamel.

Fabricator
Lunsford Signs
Granby, CO
(970) 887-3977
Designer
Joel Lunsford
Lunsford Signs
Client
Mrs. Z's Burger Barn
Selling Price
$2,200

This 5 × 5-ft. MDO and aluminum composite material sign is mounted on a custom-made, 3-in. steel, square-tube frame. The graphics were handpainted and airbrushed with 1Shot and Matthews (MAPS) paints. The "Burger Barn" copy is lettered with Gerber vinyl and the sign is coated in Frog Juice.

Fabricator
Sign Design
Wooster, OH
(330) 262-8838
Designer
Ken Stiffler
Sign Design
Client
Stebbins National Bank
Selling Price
$1,195

This sign for a century-old, family-owned bank uses a 42 × 84-in. MDO signboard. The background, borders and scrollwork are painted with 1Shot enamels, and the lettering is SparCal vinyl.

Fabricator
  Touch of Class Signs
  Jackson, NJ
  (732) 928-2102
Designer
  Joe Orbin
  Touch of Class Signs
Client
  World Karate
Selling Price
  $400

This PVC plastic sign is affixed to sheet rock with double-sided tape, and is painted with 1Shot enamels and a Badger airbrush.

Fabricator
Sign Design
Wooster, OH
(330) 262-8838
Designer
Ken Stiffler
Sign Design
Client
Mast Pharmacy
Selling Price
$1,435

This 33 × 192-in. MDO signboard has a background painted with 1Shot enamels, and SparCal letters and scrollwork.

Fabricator
Vital Signs
Pensacola, FL
(850) 434-6364

Designers
Chip Spirson
Vital Signs

Mike Kenny
Mike Kenny Adv.
Pensacola, FL
(850) 433-1972

Client
Seville Harbour Marina
& Office Complex

These sandblasted, 2-in.-thick redwood signs measure 96 × 40 in. and 60 × 48 in. They feature a Sintra® expanded PVC overlay and a frame of T-11 siding, stained deep green. Sherwin Williams and 1Shot-brand paints likewise contribute to the project's net worth. As for the signs' perch, they are mounted on 16 ft., structure-treated telephone poles.

Fabricator
MCM Graphix
Moundsville, WV
(304) 845-2825
Designers
Matthew and Crista Menard
MCM Graphix
Client
Dr. deGarmeaux
Selling Price
$2,100

Local residential codes in Moundsville, WV, limited the size of this chiropractor's sign to only 4 sq. ft. Since the Menards, signmakers at MCM Graphix, couldn't bend the rules when creating this display, they stretched their imaginations. Made in five layers, the double-sided, dimensional sign features a handcut frame; carved, beveled edges; a sandblasted panel; and a handcarved banner with sandblasted lettering. The handcut, sculpted main copy incorporates 23K goldleaf and an inset border. Enamel paints used on the sign match colors on the chiropractor's house. Regarding installation, the sign is inserted into a 1-in.-wide, routed slot in the 4 × 6-in. cedar post.

Fabricators
Innovative Sign Group
Richardson, TX
(972) 671-7155

Cutting Edge Signs
Arlington, TX
(817) 419-8847
Designer
Lyon Adv.
Austin, TX
(512) 480-5966
Client
David Bagwell Co.
Selling Price
$2,500

Balanced layout is the seed of quality sign design, and this project certainly has that. Mounted between custom, fluted 6 × 6-in. posts, the sign face is fabricated using ½ in. Lusterboard® aluminum-faced panels and industrial electrostatic paint. The leaves and acorns are made of Precision Board high-density urethane and feature airbrushed accents.

Fabricators
Sign Classics
New Paltz, NY
(914) 256-9133

Rocking Horse Ranch
Highland, NY
(914) 691-2927

Designers
Joan Schuman & Assoc.
Kingston, NY
(914) 338-2955

Brian Kurzius
Sign Classics

Client
Rocking Horse Ranch

Selling Price
$7,000 (Does not include base.)

Hand-carved with cut-out letters using high-density urethane, this 4 × 15-ft.
sign was designed using Sign Wizard CAS software. The horse logo was
both handcarved and sandblasted.

Fabricator
MCM Graphix
Moundsville, WV
(304) 845-5825

Designers
Matthew and Crista Menard
MCM Graphix

Client
Vineyard Christian Fellowship

This 4 × 8-ft. sign includes columns made with five layers of 1½-in. Sign•Foam® over 4 × 6-in. posts. The columns and raised areas on the sign were given a stucco finish with TSF 45 by Coastal Enterprises. The "Vineyard" copy and the grapes are hand carved and finished with glossy enamel, and outlined with copper. The grape leaf is fabricated from copper sheeting and finished with a green patina.

Fabricator
Sundance Sign & Design Co.
Dover, NH
(603) 742-1517

Designers
Mike Leary and Jill Butterfield
Sundance Sign & Design Co.

Client
Güldies

To give this double-faced, 48 × 92-in. Sign•Foam® high-density urethane sign a dimensional look, Sundance Sign Co. sandblasted the substrate using a GrainFraim device. The "Güldies" copy is handcarved, appliquéd, high-density urethane lettering. Porter paint, Deka sign enamel and copperleaf contribute to the color and vibrancy of the sign's simulated stained-glass border.

Fabricators
Sign Crafters
San Marcos, TX
(512) 392-0900

Precision Signs
New Braunfels, TX
(830) 606-9700

Designer
Suzanne Sessions Inc.
St. Louis
(314) 241-2355

Client
Sea World of Texas

A pair of signs mark the two entrances to the park's newest "hypercoaster." The eel figure is ¼-in. plate aluminum, rolled to form a figure-8. The "steel eel" copy are two layers of ½-in. plate aluminum, stacked on top of each other, and pegged off the body of the eel figure. The copy and figure are painted by hand, and the artificial coral was added by the park to complete the underwater illusion.

Dimensional Signs: Mounted

Fabricator
Willow Lake Design
Bayfield, Ontario
(519) 565-2900

Designer
Pete Payne
Willow Lake Design

Client
Goderich Skin Essentials

Selling Price
$3,975 (Includes glue-chipped front
windows and camera-ready artwork.)

Cut and carved from 15-lb. Sign•Foam high-density urethane, the large
lettering and the woman's face are finished with Jay Cooke-brand
primer, 1Shot paint and two shades of matte Frog Juice glaze. Two-mil
Avery vinyl is used for the sign's secondary message. The shop's glass
windows and door are glue-chipped and gilded.

Fabricator
Sign It Signs
Cornwall, Ontario
(613) 933-7447
Designers
Nancy Beaudette and Nöella Cotnam
Sign It Signs
Client
The Stork Club

Measuring 30 × 18 in., the Stork Club sign comprises a sandblasted panel with dimensional scrolls and letters. Handcarved in Sign•Foam high-density urethane, the bird is painted in acrylics. The Stork Club cameo is handcarved with attached gilded letters; copperleaf is used on the stripe around the sign's inner edge.

Fabricator
Skyline Design
Chicago
(773) 278-4660
Designer
Skyline Design
Client
Burger King — Chicago
Selling Price
$30,000

The display marks the entrance of a themed Chicago Burger King whose decorative interior elements pay homage to the American working class. Measuring 4 × 8 ft., this whopper of a sign is made of handcarved foam and fiberglass, and incorporates a metallic-painted finish and a matte protective sealer.

Fabricator
  GW Graphics
  Kelowna, British Columbia
  (250) 763-5906
Designer
  Gene Weisbeck
  GW Graphics
Client
  GW Graphics

Not only were paint and chisels used in this sign's fabrication, they were used in its design. Measuring 8 × 5 ft., the cedar sign is handcarved with a sandblasted interior. GW Graphics used a scrollsaw to cut the display's 1-in. Sign•Foam high-density urethane letters before finishing them in aluminum leaf. The 3-in.-thick top characters are also carved from Sign•Foam, while a Precix router was used to engrave the display panel.

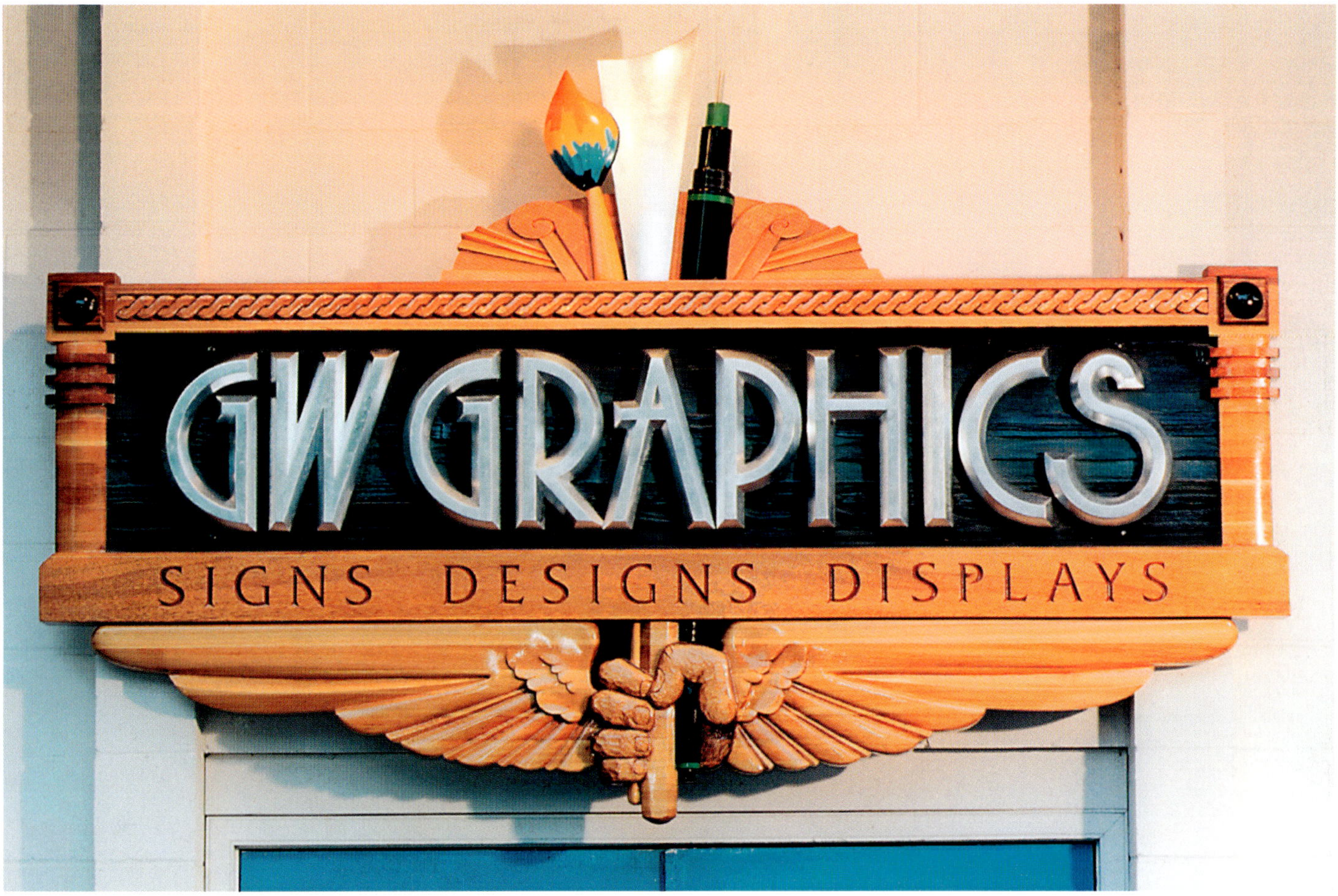

Fabricator
ARTeffects Inc.
Bloomfield, CT
(860) 242-0031
Designers
Sonalist Inc.
Waterford, CT
(860) 442-4355

ARTeffects Inc.
Client
Mohegan Sun

This projecting sign measures
4 × 8 ft., is fabricated from aluminum, and is sprayed with a
rust-colored patina finish. The
Indian figure inset is carved
from Sign•Foam and hand
painted. The "clay pipe" copy is
gold leaf; "smokes" and the
details are routed acrylic. The
logs around the border are
wrapped with leather straps.

Fabricator
Sign It Signs
Cornwall, Ontario
(613) 933-7447
Designers
Nancy Beaudette and
Nöella Cotnam
Sign It Signs
Client
Ben Moss Jewellers

This dimensional store sign features a
prismatic gilded logo and ½-in. MDF
letters installed on a contoured frame

Fabricator
  Sign It Signs
  Cornwall, Ontario
  (613) 933-7447
Designers
  Nancy Beaudette and Nöella Cotnam
  Sign It Signs
Client
  McDonald Duncan

The dimensional letters are 1-in. Sign•Foam cut on a Sabre 408 and rounded in the center by hand. The letters are gilded with 23K gold and mounted to ½-in. black PVC. The blind justice icon background is routed, ½-in. Sign•Foam, and the figure itself is also gilded with 23K gold. The sign measures 17 × 3 ft. overall.

Fabricator
LA Signs & Graphics
Burbank, CA
(818) 841-9565
Designer
John Studden
LA Signs & Graphics
Client
Promenade Services
Selling Price
$2,000 per panel

With a little help from John Studden, the days of selling food from aluminum boxes comes to an end with these stunning gilded glass signs designed for high-end mahogany and brass vendor carts. These vintage street-advertising masterpieces incorporate screenprinted graphics and reverse-painting techniques, in addition to the gilding. The background is carved from high-density urethane with a router and finished with automotive paints.

Fabricator
Sign Design
Wooster, OH
(330) 262-8838
Designer
Ken Stiffler
Sign Design
Client
Mast Pharmacy
and Card Shop
Selling Price
$545

Ken Stiffler combined Mike Jackson's (Jackson, WY) decorative scrollwork with his own type artistry to create these retro graphic gems for a local pharmacy chain.

The type started as the standard Tiffany font included with FlexiSIGN-PRO®, but Ken, no stranger to custom logos, heavily modified the font to give it a special look for the client.

The SparCal vinyl was cut on a Graphtec FC2100 and installed at all of the pharmacy locations, where the hometown feel of the work has drawn compliments from customers.

Fabricator
Adventure Adv.
Camden, ME
(207) 236-8049
Designer
Joseph Ryan
Adventure Adv.
Client
Market on Main
Selling Price
$350

Starting from a rough sketch on a napkin provided by the client, Joseph Ryan created these minimal, yet eye-catching, window treatments. Universal-brand cast vinyl was printed on a Roland ColorCAMM printer to create the finished graphic.

Fabricator
E. Quigley and Co.
Kilkenny, Ireland
+353 56 23828
Designer
Eóin Quigley
E. Quigley and Co.
Client
Kieran Campion Dental
Laboratory
Selling Price
$1,600

The glass measures 40 × 26 in., and is glue chipped and acid etched with mica chips. The blends on the border and oval are mixtures of 24K, 18K and 12K gold. The border, oval and "1 hour" copy are acid etched. The watch crystals are gilded with 18K gold. The copy "denture" and "services" have 24K bright lines, black outlines, and spun moon gold centers. The "repair" copy is individually made mother-of-pearl letters with black outline on a 24K gilded, glue-chipped field. Fine Gold's Backup is used on the backing and outlines, and 1Shot Quick Drying Gold Size is used on the moon spun gold.

Fabricator
Donovan Design Studio
Woodstown, NJ
(856) 769-2471
Designer
Samuel M. Donovan
Donovan Design Studio
Client
Millville Army Air Field Museum
Selling Price
$32,500

The Millville Army Airfield was a training airbase during WWII. This mural is a memorial dedicated to the 14 men who died at the base during training. The mural, executed on the front brick façade of the Millville City Hall, consists of three panels: two 10 × 40-ft. side panels and a 20 × 40-ft. center panel. The top of the mural is 70 ft. above the ground. Completed on Jan. 2, 1998, the mural was executed with Sherwin Williams cold-weather paints and overcoated with Aquarius 3000 anti-graffiti coating.

Designers
Michael C. Burns IV
Erin Holubeck
Master Graphics Design Studio
Cincinnati, OH
(513) 272-9279

Client
City of Cincinnati

Selling Price
$22,500 (Donated to city)

Designed to hide restoration of Cincinnati's historic Tyler Davidson Fountain, this 2,500-sq.-ft. mural provides background about the fountain itself and the restoration project. The mural was designed using Adobe Photo-Shop and Illustrator software with photographs taken by the designers. The fabrication uses 3M Scotchprint on vinyl mounted on Sintra™ board.

Wall Murals/Supergraphics

Fabricator
Donovan Design Studio
Woodstown, NJ
(856) 769-2471
Designer
Samuel M. Donovan
Donovan Design Studio
Client
Benderson Development
Selling Price
$85,000

If you can't get lakefront real estate for your development, this mural provides the next best solution. The 39 × 200-ft. mural was executed using Sherwin Williams exterior acrylic on Dri-vit™ with a protective layer of Aquarius 3000 anti-graffiti overcoat.

All subject matter for the mural was taken from the local area. The mural's five panels represent wilderness, recreation, the residential community, government and industry. All are connected through the theme of the Egg Harbor River. The overall symbolism of the arch connects the new economic center of the community with the old center, which can be viewed through the arches. Sam Donovan reported he spent more than 1,600 hours over a period of four months to complete this work.

Fabricator
Sign It Signs
Cornwall, Ontario, Canada
(613) 933-7477

Designers
Nancy Beaudette
Noella Cotnam
Sign It Signs

Client
Laura's Flowers

To satisfy this client's desire for an asymmetrical approach to sign design, Sign It painted this wall mural using exterior acrylics on the stucco outside wall of this flower shop.

Fabricator
Adamany Art and Design
Rockford, IL
(815) 961-0774

Designer
Mark J. Adamany
Adamany Art and Design

Client
Firehouse Pub

This 7 × 23-ft. sign is painted with Muralo "Deep Vogue" acrylic enamels.

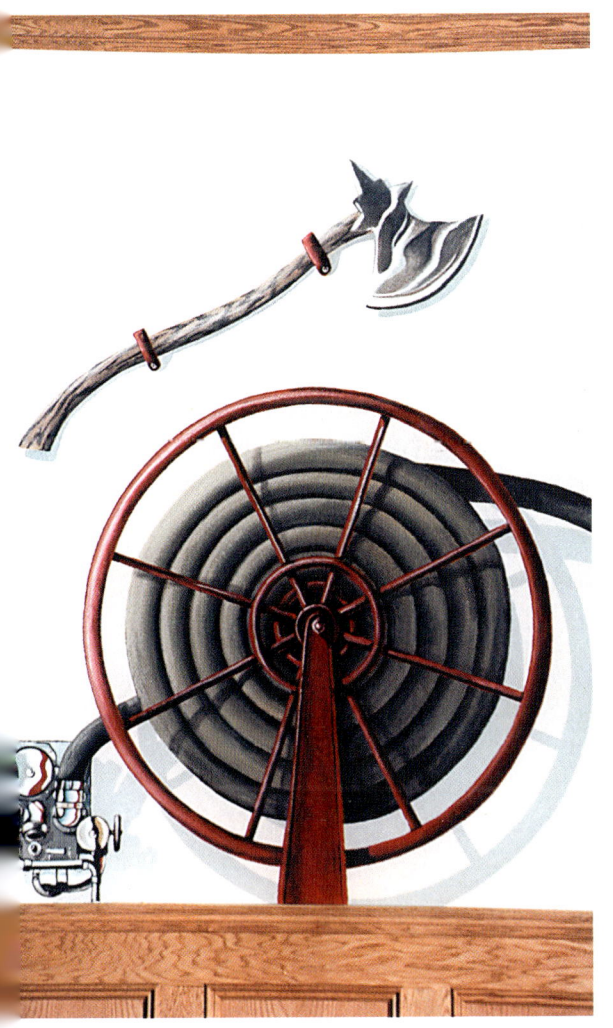

Fabricator
  Lombardo Graphics
  N. Andover, MA
  (978) 688-1230
Window engraving
  Engraving by Schlos
Designer
  David Lombardo
Client
  Owner's sign shop van

Intended to mimic the '70s van craze, these vehicle graphics were designed for self-promotion. The mural was entirely airbrushed using House of Kolor urethane. Lombardo used Gerber Edge® to digitally print the boy (his son), dog and the mountain graphics. The entire van was then cleared with House of Kolor urethane.

Fabricator
MCM Graphix
Moundsville, WV
(304) 845-2825
Designers
Matthew and Crista Menard
MCM Graphix
Client
Demerski
Selling Price
$350

The white copy is airbrushed using Createx Auto Air paints. Metallic gold vinyl with a black vinyl drop-shadow is used for the lettering, while Roland's Color-Camm was used to create the digitally-printed pictorial. The entire work is clearcoated with Frog Juice.

Fabricator
Cranberry Signcraft
Mattapoisett, MA
(508) 758-9692

Designer
Karen Souza
Cranberry Signcraft

Client
D. Lawrence Trucking

The 22K Florentine Sign Gold lettering and scrolls with split and blended shades accentuate the maroon "bagged" oval backing. Cranberry also used three-color striping with hand-cut Sign Gold "fillers" made with Gerber Graphix Advantage® software and 1Shot paints.

Fabricator
Signs by Smith
Ruidoso Downs, NM
(505) 378-8434
Designers
Don Smith
Jimmy Smith
Nick Herrera, fire chief
Client
Ruidoso Downs Fire
Department
Selling Price
$800

This fire department SUV's graphics were designed using Pro Vehicle Outlines from Digital Auto Library and Sign Wizard Grand software. They were cut out of SparCal vinyl on a SummaGraphic D15 Plotter. The vinyls used were SparCal 1229 orange engineering-grade reflective, SparCal 1228 new gold engineer grade reflective, and SparCal 1500 black premium high performance. All graphics were applied dry.

Commercial Vehicle Graphics

Fabricator
   Peach Signs
   Sandwich, MA
   (508) 477-0500
Designer
   Bob Peach
   Peach Signs
Client
   Peach Signs Shop Truck

This signshop truck demonstrates a wide range of materials and techniques. The basecoat, flames and clearcoat are DuPont chrome illusion graphics, the dimensional peach is Sign•Foam with 22K gold leaf and 1Shot enamel, and the copy is Calon vinyl and 22K SignGold. The lettering was designed and cut on an Anagraph plotter.

Fabricator
MCM Graphix
Moundsville, WV
(304) 845-2825

Designer
Matthew and Crista Menard
MCM Graphix

Client
Kitten Hill Farm

Selling Price
$250

Calon HP vinyl comprises the lettering, accents and horse logo for this sign. All gradient parts of this graphic are sprayed with Krylon paint and clearcoated with Frog Juice.

Fabricator
Touch of Class Signs
Jackson, NJ
(732) 928-2102

Designer
Joe Orbin
Touch of Class Signs

Client
Monmouth Aerial

Selling Price
$1000

This old-time flying tiger P-40 plane found itself grounded and gritting its teeth in the War Plane Museum (Wall Township, NJ), but was flying high when painted with 1Shot lettering and enamel.

Fabricator
Jutras Signs
Manchester, NH
(603) 622-2344
Designer
Chris R. Joyce
Jutras Signs
Client
George Sweeney
Selling Price
$590

This flaming hot rod with an exposed engine makes for one hot ride. The flames were designed with Gerber Graphix Advantage® 6.2 and executed on the Gerber Edge. The two-spot colors were painted on clear enamel.

Fabricator
Sign Concepts
Addison, IL
(630) 495-7446

Designers
Al and Lynda Bolek
Sign Concepts

Client
Hemingway's
Restaurant and Bar

This restaurant and bar uses a 4 × 8-ft., 11-oz.,
Sign-Tex enamel-receptive banner to entice its visitors.
The sign's large text is handpainted using 1Shot
paint; the small text is produced from Spar-Cal vinyl.

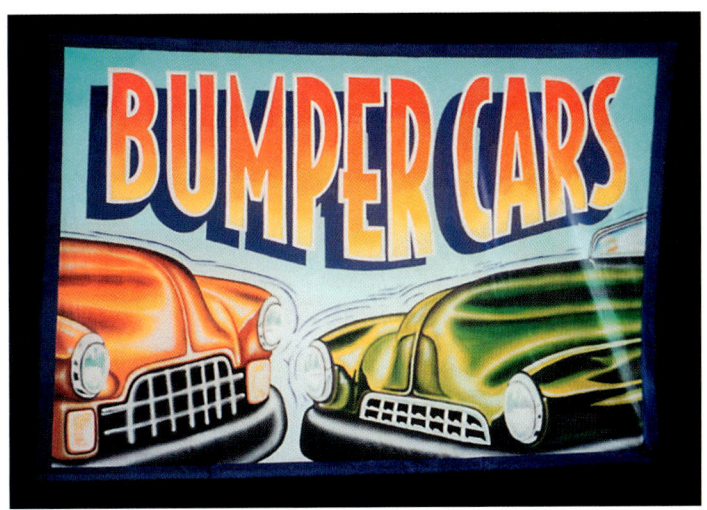

Fabricator
Great Big Signs
Kyle, TX
(512) 262-2157
Designer
Lynn Wilkerson
Great Big Signs
Client
Gatti Land

The artwork for these banners was designed using Corel 8. The banners themselves are hand-sewn muslin with Ronan Primall Primer, and hand lettered with 1Shot enamels. Ronan Flat Vinyl Cote Clear is the protective coat. The banners average 5 × 12 ft. in size.

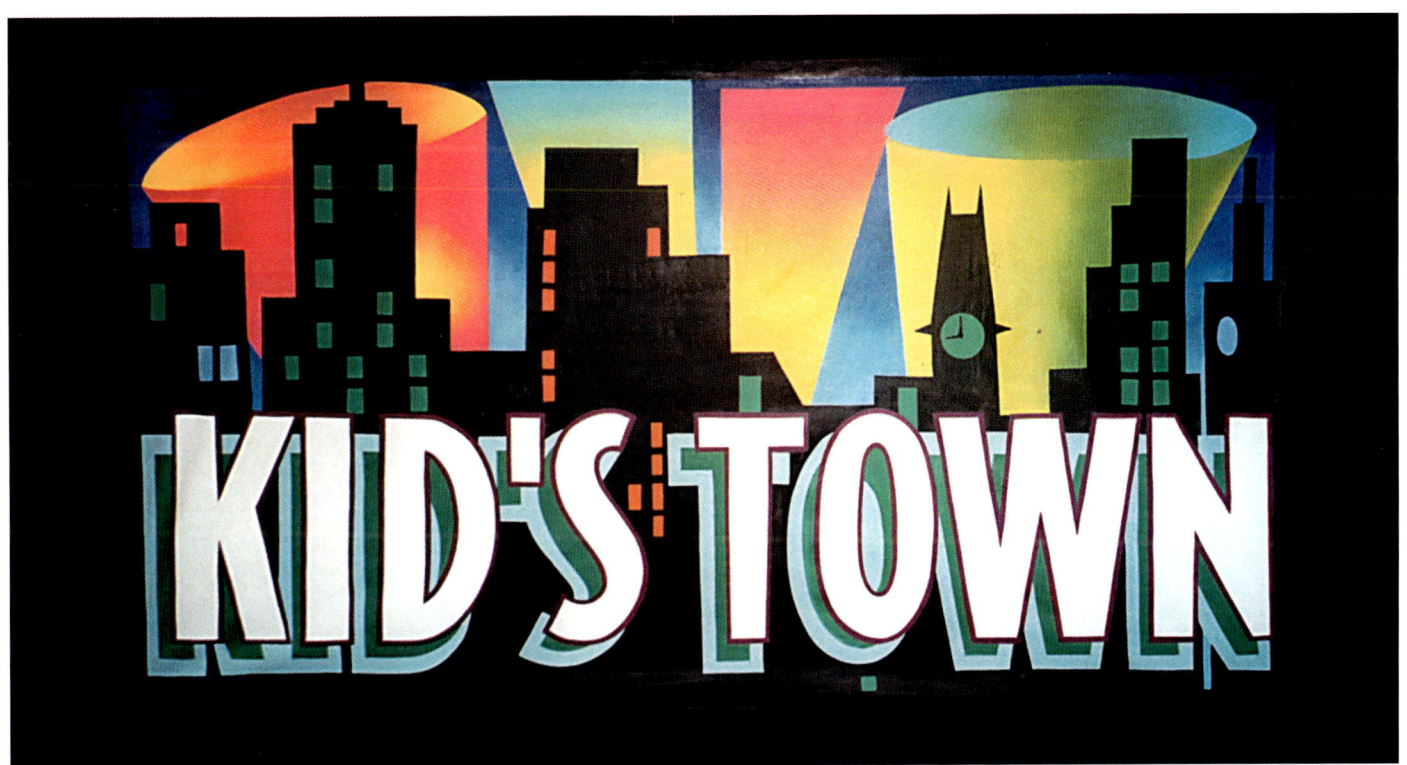

Fabricator
Vital Signs
Pensacola, FL
(850) 434-6364
Designer
Karyn Spirson
Vital Signs
Client
J.G. Interiors
Selling Price
$600

This canvas banner painted with Sherwin Williams paint measures 72 × 60 in., and its style represent old-fashioned circus art.

Fabricator
MCM Graphix
Moundsville, WV
(304) 845-2825
Designers
Matthew and Crista Menard
MCM Graphix
Client
West Virginia State Penitentiary

Produced for a tourist attraction, this 4 × 10-ft. banner incorporates cut-vinyl and airbrushed letters on a 13-oz. vinyl substrate. "Mock Prison Riot" is airbrushed for a prismatic look; the sign's right-hand-side gold panel is airbrushed to achieve a metallic look. Krylon paint is used to create the banner's background vinyl strips.

Fabricator
Sign Concepts
Addison, IL
(630) 495-7446
Designers
Al and Lynda Bolek
Sign Concepts
Client
Barnelli's Pasta Bowl

This 3 × 8-ft. banner features 1Shot lettering enamel on 2mm vinyl.

Fabricator
Douglas Williams Wood Carving
Honolulu
(808) 597-1710

Designer
AM Partners Inc.
Honolulu
(808) 526-2828

Client
Foodland Super Market

Selling Price
$40,000

The signage for Foodland Super Market feature dimensional letters fabricated from DuPont's Corian composite material and also incorporate handpainted pin lines. The signs' other dimensional elements comprise handcarved 18-lb. Sign•Foam high-density urethane. Medex high-density composite board is used to create the structures' layered backgrounds.

Fabricator
Innovative Sign Group
Richardson, TX
(972) 671-7155

Designer
Madden Marketing &
Design Group
Richardson, TX
(972) 671-6627

Client
Duke Inc.

Selling Price
$38,000

Property stone was used to build the 7-ft.-tall, double-faced monument shown below. The structure's aluminum sign face, which measures 4 × 8 ft., features a pewter-metallic finish. Pin-raised and flat aluminum make up the sign's logo and graphics. The column caps — made from shaped aluminum with a brushed-stroke finish — support mounted pewter-painted weathervanes.

Secondary sign elements include interior aluminum structures incorporating vinyl graphics and brushed pewter paint. Signposts are composed of aluminum.

Fabricator
Natural Graphics Inc.
Houston
(713) 661-5075
Designer
Carol Pickens
Natural Graphics Inc.
Client
The Morgan Group
Selling Price
$32,000

This sign system's 8 × 5-ft. double-faced, limestone main-identification sign was created to maintain the Clear Lake apartment community's tropical theme. An applied stone plaque with beveled edges comprises the structure's logo. The tiled-pattern border is stone-etched and painted two shades of peach.

The system's secondary package incorporates both limestone and faux-finished sign faces; etched, painted posts to create dimensionality; and tiled borders.

Fabricator
  Pilot Graphics Inc.
  Alpharetta, GA
  (770) 664-0213
Designers
  W. Todd Vaught
  Michael Neiswander
  Sky Design
  Atlanta
  (404) 688-4702
Client
  JDN Realty Corp.
Selling Price
  $10,000

Affixed to the side of the building are 36-in. channel letters and a 36-in. fiberglass sphere. The 6 × 4-ft. directory sign uses Coke-bottle plexiglas with "etched" vinyl. Underneath the plex is routed 359 aluminum.

Fabricators
Dennis Punt
Gregg Akin
Rich DeSantis
Boyd Design Group
Englewood, CO
(303) 761-5741

Designers
Cecil E. Burns
Jeff Gathercole
Jim deRoin
Andrew Trunfio
Boyd Design Group

Client
Bill Stewart

Selling Price
$40,000

This festive, brightly colored resort in St. Lucia, West Indies, demanded a sign system as colorful as the buildings themselves. Each village has its own identity, marked by different characters. The main village signs are sandblasted urethane foam panels with hand-carved, hand-painted characters. The directional signs are constructed of aluminum and are fully functioning windmills.

Fabricator
Designage Inc.
Apopka, FL
(407) 884-6600

Designer
Paramount Parks Design &
Entertainment
Charlotte, NC

Client
Titanic "The Movie On Tour"

It's no accident these riveting 11-ft tall letters were used to greet guests to a 15,000-sq.-ft traveling exhibit that displayed props and memorabilia from the blockbuster movie. Fabricated in MDO with a faux finish to simulate the aged finish of the ship's hull, this gigantic attraction was backed by a 100-ft. digital vinyl print of the North Atlantic Ocean.

Fabricator
ASI
Norcross, GA
(770) 448-2026

Designers
Adriana Blandford
Thom Williams
Sky Design
Atlanta
(404) 688-4702

Client
OPUS Woods
office park

Selling Price
$34,000

This monumental entry pylon stands 10 ft. tall with three 10-ft. sides. The bottom half is bush-hammered, pre-cast stone, while the top is polished Carnelian Red granite thin-set on concrete block with etched silver lithochrome copy.

Fabricators
LNI Custom Mfg.
Hawthorne, CA
(310) 978-2000

Fireform Porcelain
Enamel Co.
Santa Rosa, CA
(707) 523-0580

Designer
Sussman/Prejza
Culver City, CA
(310) 836-3939

Client
Valley Crest

Selling Price
$147,000

Custom-fabricated porcelain enamel signs with screened graphics throughout Hancock Park direct guests passing through to Los Angeles County Museum of Art and the Page Museum, curators of the famous archeological and tourist trap.

Fabricators
Innovative Sign Group
Richardson, TX
(972) 671-7155

Gemini Inc.
Cannon Falls, MN
(800) 538-8377

Designers
Paul Fulks
and Paul Marcum
Innovative Sign Group

Client
Metric Property Mgmt.

Selling Price
$12,800

This V-shaped entry monument is 5 ft., 6 in. tall, and 10 ft. wide, and comprised of flagstone with cast stone accents. The columns and "CWB" logo are aluminum. The sign face is also aluminum with copper patina and gemini letters. The logo and crown structure were routed on a Gerber Sabre.

Fabricator
  WoodGraphics Inc.
  Douglasville, GA
  (770) 942-0688
Designer
  WoodGraphics Inc.
Client
  Exxell Developers

The size of the sign face is 4 ft., 6 in. × 9 ft. The logo and graphics are prismatic carved and gilded Sign•Foam. Black granite tile squares make up the background. The rock monument was fabricated by the client and its column caps are synthetic stucco (painted) as is the header. The elk statue was purchased by the client at an auction.

Fabricator
Garfield Signs & Graphics
Greer, SC
(864) 848-0911
Designer
Garfield Signs & Graphics
Client
Burdette's Hardware
Selling Price
$13,650

The tape measure is a 7 × 7-ft., aluminum cabinet with dimensional Sintra letters with reflective black vinyl faces. Designed with Scanvec Inspire, CorelDRAW and Scanvec Enroute, it was machined with a Multicam 48plus. The SparCal and Calon engineer grade reflective vinyl was cut using a Zeta CP3015B.

The 2000 Summer Olympics in Sydney, Australia were not only a showcase for athletics, but for event signage of all kinds as well. The challenges were many, from directing visitors from varied cultural and language backgrounds around the events and the city, to tastefully advertising the sponsors' products. *Signs of the Times*, the world leader in sign information, engaged the services of photographer Barry Allen to capture on film the widely varying forms of signs, wayfinding systems, flags and banners, car, bus and train wraps, information kiosks, awnings, posters, and high-rise building graphics. This following special section presents a sample of the signs of the 2000 Sydney Summer Olympics.

Sign design and fabrication books and videos available from ST Publications

Atkinson Reproduced in Color
Atkinson Sign Painting
Carving Signs
Commercial Sign Techniques: Step-by-Step
Complete Guide to Truck Lettering, Pinstriping and Graphics
Engineering Sign Structures: An Introduction to Analysis and Design
Gold Leaf Techniques 4th Edition
Gráficos de Vinilo
In-Store Signage & Graphics: Connecting with Your Customer
Introduction to Neon (video)
ISA Pumping Video
Mastering Layout
Neon with Craig Kraft (video)
Neon World
Neon Techniques 4th Edition
Neon: The Next Generation
New Let There Be Neon
Sign Design and Layout
Sign Design Gallery 2
Sign Gallery
Sign Gallery International
Sign Structures and Foundations
Sign User's Guide: A Marketing Aid
Stallcup's Electric Signs and Outline Lighting Book
Vinyl Graphics How-to: Master Principles
Vinyl Graphics & Auto Decor Video Instruction Series
You Are Here: Graphics that Direct, Explain & Entertain

For a complete catalog of books, videos and related educational products, contact:

ST Publications Inc.
407 Gilbert Avenue
Cincinnati, Ohio 45202
USA
Tel. 800-421-1321, 513-421-2050
Fax 513-421-6110, 513-421-5144
E-mail: books@stpubs.com
Web: www.stpubs.com/books